MATRIX

Borgo Press Books by MICHAEL R. COLLINGS

All Calm, All Bright: Christmas Offerings
The Art and Craft of Poetry: Twenty Exercises Toward Mastery
Brian Aldiss
Dark Transformations: Deadly Visions of Change
The Films of Stephen King
GemLore: An Introduction to Precious and Semi-Precious Gemstones
The House Beyond the Hill: A Novel of Horror
In Endless Morn of Light: Moral Freedom in Milton's Universe
In the Void: Poems of Science Fiction, Myth and Fantasy, & Horror
The Many Facets of Stephen King
Matrix: Echoes of Growing Up West
Naked to the Sun: Dark Visions of Apocalypse
The Nephiad: An Epic Poem in XII Books
Piers Anthony
Scaring Us to Death: The Impact of Stephen King on Popular Culture
Singer of Lies: A Science Fantasy Novel
Tales Through Time: Poems, Revised and Enlarged Edition
Toward Other Worlds: Perspectives on John Milton, C. S. Lewis, Stephen King, Orson Scott Card, and Others
Wer Means Man, and Other Tales of Terror and Wonder
Wordsmith, Part One: The Veil of Heaven: A Science Fantasy Novel
Wordsmith, Part Two: The Thousand Eyes of Flame: A Science Fantasy Novel

MATRIX

ECHOES OF GROWING UP WEST

by

Michael R. Collings

Emeritus Professor of English
Seaver College
Pepperdine University

THE BORGO PRESS

An Imprint of Wildside Press LLC

MMX

Borgo Laureate Series
ISSN 1082-3336

Number Six

Copyright © 1990, 1993, 1994, 1995, 2007, 2010 by Michael R. Collings

All rights reserved.
No part of this book may be reproduced in any form without the expressed written consent of the author and publisher.
Printed in the United States of America.

www.wildsidebooks.com

SECOND EDITION, REVISED AND ENLARGED

Table of Contents

INTRODUCTION, by W. Gregory Stewart 11

MATRIX

    M 19

I. WE LIVE IN IT STILL

    Legacy I 22
    Maternity Home 25
    On First Seeing My Photograph as a Six-Month Child 27
    Summer, 1953 28
    Going a Mile a Minute 29
    The Passing of the Old Guard 31
    Heritage 32
    At the Crick 34
    After Chores 35
    Grandmother's Attic 36
    Bathing in the Great Tin Tub 38
    Betrayal 41
    The House We Owned 42
    Sledding in Montana 43
    Snow Draperies 45
    An Act of Contrition 46
    Summer Stanzas 47
    How to Make Raspberry Syrup 48
    Melmac 50

Tornado Weather in Montana, 1959 52
1959 54
We Built Forts 57
They Had a Dream: 1959 58
Into Bread 60
The Tractor 61
Into the Forest 62
Classical Music 63
Fuchsias and Bleeding-Hearts 64
Monolith: The Tale and the Teller 65
The Road 67
Her Journals 69
For My Son 70
Clapboard Memory 72
Anamnesis I 74
Anamnesis II 76

II. TODAY

Legacy II 78
Today 83
Free Agency 85
Entire Unto Himself 86
Father-Child 87
He Is Not in the Valley 88
Childless 90
Whispers 91
Bud Died 92
I Owe My Father Much 94
Alone, in the Chapel, at the Console 95
It's Hot and Sweaty Work 96
Remembering the First Photograph of a Survivor 97
Janusaries 98
Just to Say 100
First Apricot 101
Tulips 103
Cleaning the Garage 104

Apricots This Year 105
Wind and Stone 106
Making Love at Midnight 108
The Pigeon Woman in Cooley Park 110
Bank of Virgins! 117
Shipwrecked Among the Channel Islands 118
Ritual 120
Sparks 121
I, Homeless 123
Damon Again 124
After Thirty Years of Teaching 126
Portrait of the Artist on the Verge of Middle Age 127
For Grace Isabella 129
Quilting 131
I Have Time 133

III. MEMORIES OF APPLEBUDS

I Have Seen the Mountain 136
Morning Bells 138
Applebuds Assault Slick Pewter Mist 139
Morning Glories 140
Choosing Irises 141
Bartlett Pears 143
Beyond the Harvest 144
Restoration 145
Cambria Shoreline 146
The Irrigation Ditch Lies Dead 148
Nestling 149
Off-Shore Flow 153
The Tyranny of Equilibrium 154
Walnut Harvest 156
Weeding in the Poetry Beds 157
Continuity 158

IV. The Warren Poems

Warren—Portrait of the Artist as a Neurotic 163
Warren, Dressed as a Sunbeam 164
Warren Sleeps Over 165
Warren's Mother Brings Him Water 166
Warren Travels with His Father 167
Warren Dreams While Sleeping Outside During a Heat
    Wave 169
Warren Recalls—Molestation 170
Warren Discovers Classical Music 172
Warren and Greg Talk 173
Warren Goes Camping 174
Warren Opens a Closet in the Attic 176
Warren Returns to the Homestead 178
Warren Remembers the Chicken Coop 180
Warren Relives Sierra Fires 182
Warren Plants a New Garden 183
Warren Answers a Telephone Call from Greg 184
Warren Harvests a Beefsteak Tomato 185
Warren Considers Patriphobia 186
Warren, in Therapy Today 187
Warren Evaluates the Effects of Aripiprazole 188
Warren's Mother Sells the House 189
Warren Says Farewell to His Father's Ghost 191

INDEX OF FIRST LINES 193
INDEX OF TITLES 197
ABOUT THE AUTHOR 201

ACKNOWLEDGMENTS

Grateful acknowledgment is made to the following publications in which some of the poems in *Matrix* first appeared:

Ariel XIV (Triton College, 1995); *California State Poetry Society Newsletter*; *Dialogue: A Journal of Mormon Thought*; *Earth Words: Write for Life*, Volume I (1994); *Echoes*; *Expressionist* (Pepperdine University); *Highbeams* (Beloit University Internet); *In the West of Ireland: A Literary Celebration in Contemporary Poetry*, 1994 (Ireland, 1994); *Latter-day Women*; *Latter-day Digest*; *Mobius*; *Naked to the Sun: Dark Visions of Apocalypse* (1990, 2007); *Next Phase*; *Peck Rd. Magazine*; *LA Poetry*; *Poet Magazine*; *Suisun Valley Review*; *Sunstone*; *Tongues of Fire—Write for Life*, Volume II (Write for Life, 1993); *Zarahemla: A Forum for LDS Poetry*.

Poems in this collection have received the following awards:

"Going a Mile a Minute": Winner, 1995 Triton College Salute to the Arts. "Making Love at Midnight": First Place, 1994 Phantom Press Poetry Competition. "The Pigeon Woman of Cooley Park" (Part XI): Winner, 1995 Triton College Salute to the Arts. "In Therapy Today": Winner, 1993 Triton College Salute to the Arts.

For

Satya Elizabeth Gratner
who so masterfully edited the
first edition of
Matrix

And, as always, for

Judi—
After over thirty-five years, still my finest
audience and critic

INTRODUCTION

TO THE FIRST EDITION OF *MATRIX*

Michael shows us himself in order to touch us; and
he touches us to show us ourselves.

I have known Dr. Michael R. Collings since 1989. He is warm, wholesome, and delightful—as well as erudite, lucid, and well-versed in an area at which I only dabble as an amateur. And in *Matrix* I get to know him better; and surprisingly (or maybe not so…), I think I get to know myself a little better, too. Because in this volume, he writes to us all—and he touches each of us who might have ever been at all human and happy or human and frail or human and fearful or human in love.

This collection, following the prefatory and powerful "M," is an assemblage in 4 parts, a symphony in 4 movements, a feast with 4 courses—let us nibble ….

WE LIVE IN IT STILL

Here is where you taste warm bread after chores or explore Grandmother's Attic. Here, too, is where you discover that Michael appreciates form as well as freedom, and recognizes that sometimes, the better part of license is understatement.

My favorite poem from this section—and possibly from the entire collection—is "For My Son."

Now, I have never been able to properly put to paper my feelings for my own son. When I try, I fail—Jesse is a miracle beyond whatever skills I hold. In "For My Son," Michael gently touches his own miracle in a way that I wish I could—gently, eloquently, lovingly, and with a sense of generations and the ages.

> And once I held him small and felt him
> Small and heard him small
> And wonderful….

I wept to read this piece.

And smiled.

Today

Possibly the most important piece in TODAY is "The Pigeon Woman in Cooley Park." This is Michael's "Howl." But it is a howl wearied and spent, and howling not so much to rant as to remember. It is the careful howl of this time and this place, after the storm and before the race…a howl of experience.

Memory of Applebuds

Michael writes in "Cambria Shoreline"

> God not yet
> finished
> blending green to gray

There is something sly here—as much as this section seems to cry out "return to nature," there is something else whispering parenthetically: "If you can." "The Irrigation Ditch Lies Dead," for example, sneaks up on you, and by the time it taps you on the shoulder, you're already into the bittersweet of "Nestling" and beyond.

THE WARREN POEMS

It's a pleasure just reading the titles of this section—"Warren, Dressed as a Sunbeam," "Warren Sleeps Over," "Warren's Mother Brings Him Water" ... and so on.

Then, as if a tour through the titles weren't enough of a treat, we can step inside the poems, themselves.

And Michael.

And ourselves....

The final entry in this section—"Warren Says Farewell to His Father's Ghost"—brings everything full round—the section and the book—and is a finely chosen end piece. There is a consummate craftsmanship evident here, a careful sculpting, handsomely realized. And when Michael writes, in the closing lines

> Spine, caressed its softness, then slid the book again into its place upon
>
> The shelf.

You know that this volume will find its own special place upon your shelf, that you will take it down again and again, and read it again and again, and put it back, always carefully.

W. Gregory Stewart
Los Angeles

MATRIX:
ECHOES OF GROWING UP WEST

They seemed others, but are we;
Our second selves those shadows be.
	—Thomas Traherne, "Shadows in the Water"

I saw Eternity the other night
Like a great Ring of pure and endless Light,
    All calm as it was bright....
	—Henry Vaughan, "The World"

There let the pealing Organ blow
To the full voices Choir below....
	—John Milton, "Il Penseroso"

M

                                          1

A thousand wives lie close to heart,
                              intimáte,
shape shivering breasts to word-dream
           couplings,
bald lips to   consummation
in the lust
       of vividry
               and transmutation
pressing painful birth into a wilder universe
part and part and part and intimation
timbreling into
                   completion

                                2

A thousand secret selves clamor
for carved ears,
a thousand altérnate selves,
                                simmering
elementals recording what is/seems and was
and what may be—
a thousand pale prospective nightmares
      dreams
expulsive energies define
and
redefine into straw-dawn infinity

                               3

A thousand deaths thrive here
a thousand
                   apparitional

cheddar-scaled goldfish
floating in blue tepid water and
        cannibalizing
bloated skull and unzipped spine
of one that once was of their own kind
when it still lived—
        but failed
transmutation
        became
consummation
rocking on aquarial blue-plastic coated stones

       4

A thousand children sleep soundly
in typic beds—
progeny of imagery,
      heirs of rhythms
potentialities
unenfleshed and ripening
  tattering on weak
iambs

       to dream
mortality
and pungent smells
of
swollen ripeness
      pressed
in black arc-lines
against a thousand
stained sheets

I. WE LIVE IN IT STILL

LEGACY I

By all accounts my great-great-great
was
a thorough-going bastard
or so I'm told

[perhaps not literally, times being what
they were — but he apparently attempted
to procreate new generations of bastards
from Kentucky to
Kansas's frontier]

Today he would stand condemned—
    Child-abuser
    Spouse-abuser
    Obsessive-compulsive on a power-trip

    Bigot

But then he was
    a successful businessman
    a strict disciplinarian
    a conscientious provider
    who
        wore the pants in *that* family,
        no mistake—

And no one questioned occasional missteps

He raised this house.
He dug its foundations with pick and shovel,

slicing through prairie hardpan to softer strata beneath—
He sweat in July mugginess until
the fluids of his body wedded black earth
in the basement—
    unconscious pagan ritual—
    setting clotting cornerstones in
    sacrificial blood—

He built this house.
He hoisted timbers, bracing them with
gut and twisted hemp until he drove
square-forged nails through their grain.
He shored the walls and plastered inside
and out until the place shimmered
beneath the nooning sun.

He built this house—
We live here still, his great-great-greats
[a few of them, at least];

We've
    sealed earthen basement floors with six inches
    of grey concrete reinforced with rebar
We've
    rehung windows on sashes bleached grey-white—
    replaced age-rippled glass he mounted in another century,
    replaced it with crisp, durable, ecologically responsible
        smoothly invisible double-glass panes that
        improve our vision
We've
    reshingled
    repainted
    restored
                but

The house remains part him
part us—

We've sold the northeast acres to a New Age Church—
    the southwest forty for a mini-mall where clerks
    with ancient accents and exotic smiles greet faded farmers—
We've looked across truncated fields
        over hardwood fences he erected
    at neighbors who would have been

                anathema
to him and

we've held their hearts in ours and opened
    his doors to them
    and drunk with them
    from the still-sweet-flowing well
    he sank beneath the cottonwoods
    and share with them
    summer shade against the nooning sun

He built this house;
We live in it still.

Maternity Home

    For six weeks after, she remained
in the Maternity Home, washing
other mothers' dishes, setting plates
and silverware in stacks just so
on dingy shelves lined with yellowed
newspapers that carried War News
and—one, tucked far back into
a corner—lists of casualties from
forgotten years before.
    For six weeks after, she haunted
rooms and corridors between her
moments with her child; wandering
alone and quiet just one thin wall
a way from the blizzard that stranded
them both there, lost among
other strangers.
    For six weeks after, she waited for
the storms to ease, for him to cross
half a continent and bear them both
away—away to warmth and sunlight,
away from snow and frost and cold
and midnight's pain.
    For six weeks after, she hummed to me
and whispered small sweet lies that
tasted sugar on her lips, sweet syrup lies
that I now whisper to my own in
silent stretches of the day as I too wait
my six weeks after for him to come.
Both shes and I wait quietly and rock
and whisper dreams of warmth and sunlight—

one she nested in the cradle of my arm,
the other cloaked about my neck
in memory.

On First Seeing My Photograph as a Six-Month Child

Feet splayed, he sits
alone on the harsh concrete
expanse—behind him, shadowed
so severely that nothing shows
but alternating stripes
(Were they olive and gold, perhaps,
or blue and turquoise, always
her favorites). He sits.
His arms raised high as if begging
him or her or them
to bend and pick him up.
They don't—or won't—but laugh
(presumably) at antics
thought too cute, too charming
to ignore.
    And fifty
years slide by.
He sits alone, feet
tucked sedately beneath
his desk, arms raised
to touch the keyboard and res-
urrect an infant self,
a slice of shadow, a con-
crete waste, and faces
just beyond his lens.

SUMMER, 1953

I was six.
I wheeled grandma's milk cans out
To wait like patient soldiers for the cheese truck.
I strutted in a new red and blue
Corduroy cowboy suit.
                          (Korea was over—barely)
I raided raspberries,
Squishing succulence on my tongue.
I avoided alfalfa-snakes in overgrown fields.
I rode stick horses at full gallop
Across the log bridge, risking tumbles
Into nettles and polliwog-slime.
                        (Viet Nam was about to begin)
I fished for six-inch whoppers.
I slept out on a rusty spring,
Waking when a 1940s Ford
Or Chevy or Nash crunched over graveled roads.
I stared at stars, my eyes not yet myopic enough
To need corrective lenses.
                   (Sputnik was an engineer's conception)
I rode with grandpa to deliver eggs,
Flats of eggs on the back seat,
Warm-stuffy grey seat-pile in front,
A green translucent spinner on the steering wheel.
Four hours into Burley and back—
A ninety mile trip.

(The moon rose, still untouched)

Going a Mile a Minute

was a climax forty years ago—
six children crammed pre-astronautic
inside stuffy sleek-backed grey-wind lines
of the uncle's cone-nosed Studebaker

as it struggled up the gantry-gravel road
halfway between Elba and Burley
beneath a clear blue Idaho sky—
last week of vacation, last visit

to the homestead farm, last picnic up
Cripple Creek, last watermelons floating lazy
dead-man's floats in icy water
reminding shockingly of last winter's snows

still hunched on Cleveland's upper flanks—
but in the valley heat crowded the gravel road
as the uncle's Studebaker approached
the overlook—six children crushed closer

hung over the back seat almost into
the uncle's lap—heads bobbing back and forth
in urgent efforts to focus on the cyclopean
speedometer arrow-hovering at thirty-five

dropping to thirty to twenty-five to
twenty as the cloud of summer dust wailed
beneath bald tires and drifted sobbing down
the hill behind the Studebaker—

and the crest—a momentary hovering in
space before the sleek-silver woman shimmering the hood
dipped her curtsey to obsolescent gravity—and the
car slid over the edge and down down down

down between wide fields of winter wheat and
down down down and the arrow-needle
swings up and around past thirty-five again
past forty forty-five fifty-five

and the slope smoothes out to embrace
a rutted level road stretching toward
clumps of cottonwoods distant grey—
but the needle quivers upward upward

fifty-seven -eight -nine and at the climax
with a scream adumbrating "We have lift-off"
six voices pitch above the Studebaker's cranked-up
whine and deafen the uncle

with "A MILE A MINUTE! ... A MILE A MINUTE! ...
A MILE A MINUTE!" as the old car shudders
across wagon ruts and skirts fields just past
harvesting and the arrow-needle

droops exhausted down down down
to a sedate and somber thirty-five and
six children huddle in voiceless thrill against thick
stuffy grey pile and work to catch their breath

re-fill lungs with earth-bound breath
and contemplate with newly adult tenderness
the mystery and the wonder and the awe
of going a mile a minute.

The Passing of the Old Guard

Thunder rumbled through the valley;
End to end it mumbled over fields
Until it echoed in a whisper
Up Hollow Crick
And died.

It wasn't thunder. Dynamite set in the basement
Of the old stone chapel rattled granite
Blocks—burst sound to Tower Rock
And curled back to wade
Among bleak ruins.

The rocks were set by hand in concrete poured
By hand a century ago. Wood cut from
Pine a day's trek away, floors
Set piece by piece
By hand.

Dust...delayed roar...the spire collapses
Into its guts. That's all. The end.
I remember the roar, and
The steeple as
It fell.

The new brick chapel—made of yellow brick
With lead-white trim—stood only twenty
Years. Today I drove by to watch
The ball and crane
Attack and win.

Heritage

Even now the house remembers,
Even now,
After the new people have ripped and sealed,
Changed smooth log steps for harsh concrete,
Hidden the well beneath a featureless walkway,
Rooted out raspberry canes and current bushes and
Filled gaping holes
With ornamental junipers and hybrid grass
(**GUARANTEED!**
REQUIRES LESS WATER!
LITTLE MOWING!!
PRACTICALLY NO CARE!!!)

Even now the house remembers
As shadows inch along brickwork hiding
Hand-hews logs and chipped grout.
The new people think the brick
More practical, more durable
(*Remember the old Rasmussen place?*
When the wreckers came with sledges, mallets, finally a bulldozer—
    only to discover palisaded walls, three-foot foundations. They fi-
    nally had to use their dynamite.)
The attic—now three charming bedrooms
Without charm—
Still remembers unfinished beams,
Darkly silent corners enfolding
Ancient gramophones,
Dusty-mirrored dressers
Brimming with hidden treasures and musty smells,
Almost fears.
But that is only memory,

Except the dozen bluebottles
Crisp and sere on the western windowsill.
They remain,
And the house remembers.

All is gone:
Dank cellars shivered with the smell of carrots and potatoes in December; faded pink, forgotten swirls of flowers on the living room carpet; the door opening into nowhere, the six-foot drop into the pansy bed; boxelders, swings, the chicken coop)
In their place
Garden spots run to weeds,
Two iron-pink flamingos
Formed of welded reaper-blades stride
Frozen on the lawn.

Only Chimney Rock,
Squatting above the Valley,
Remains the same.

But even now, the house remembers.

AT THE CRICK

We fished for crawdads from the old plank bridge
Worn satin-smooth by balding retreads
On antique 'A's and 'T's
And scarred by horseshoes
Forged

In Grandpa's blacksmith shed. We cast our lines
Beneath deep, thickly shadowed arcs
Of willows mystery-dark
That bent to touch
Black

Water, not knowing that we had no hooks,
No bait, just sisal twine too worn
For baling this year's hay.
We sat, back-bare,
Feet

Dangling over nothingness as if
The summer's heat, the cloying dust,
The essence of our youth
Were more than fragment
Dreams.

AFTER CHORES

Warm bread broken into warm cream-
clotted milk still smelling of the cow's
warm teat, curled into thick crockery
brown-rimmed and crazed with time-

imposed discolorations, hair-fine lines
to web the gleaming bowl and seem
to hold it not it them. Rich rank cheese
crumbling golden on the plate, mockery

of butter beaten churned turned flattery
with yellow cheeks. Honey dribbled hive-
fresh thick ambrous from a clear green
cutglass pitcher a century old, a house

With arbor handle, chimney spout. Now
cinnamon hazes from the open pantry
promise pies and turnovers. Suppertime
weds bedtime, sleep wombs fragrant dreams.

Grandmother's Attic

In Grandmother's attic
    Time seemed to stand still—
        The whole world grew static
            Within its grey sills;

Fine dust of long decades
    Hung thick in dry air
        Or fell in quaint brocades
            On oak planks once bare;

Dark's deep purple fingers
    Reached out from low walls
        In shadows that lingered
            Long before sunset-fall.

BUT time-hidden treasures
    Invited young hands
        To discover lost pleasures,
            Like strange, distant lands;

A drawer frilled with laces,
    Pink ribbons, age-paled;
        An album with faces
            Grown brittle and frail;

A toddler-sized teacup
    With porcelain plate;
        Wood buttons to thread up
            On twine gray as slate.

Each corner … sweet hours
 Of diligent play;
  Each carton … a bower
   Where Time's kept at bay—

In Grandmother's attic
 Where memories thrill,
  And past years lie static—
   Where they slept … and sleep still.

Bathing in the Great Tin Tub

Bathing in the great tin tub
at Grandma's house—

Always on Saturday night, after
solemn suppers of freshly baked
bread and milk still warm from
the teat, a rich scum of cream
clotting on the bowl.

Always on Saturday night, after
dishes were scalded in water so
hot it seemed to dry at once
without our having to wipe
the mismatched china plates.

Always after Grandpa settled
in the living room behind his
paper and his seed catalogues,
his work-stiff overalls pungent
with his smell and the smell
of cattle and hard labor.

Always stripping by the wood-stoked
stove, just around its cast-iron
corner where Grandma would not see,
dropping play-worn clothing in
a pile beyond the woodbox—they
would disappear as I bathed.

Always scuttling naked across
the gray linoleum, a pinkish
beetle hunching its way
toward the great tin tub
frothy with bubbles and
steaming even in the over-heated
kitchen air.

Always slipping gingerly into
water so hot I felt it to my ears
at the first quick brush of toe,
testing, settling, choosing
uncomfortably between
the known heat of water straight
from the heavy iron pot already
heating more on the back burner and
the unknown heat of Grandma's
eyes should she turn and look
before I was completely covered.

Always shivering as the water
chilled more rapidly than I
could imagine, then
pressing against the cold tin side
as Grandma poured another
kettle of hot and stirred it
with an aged, arthritic hand.

Always shuddering as I rose,
rose-pink and small and naked
in the sudden kitchen chill
and wrapped in oven-warmed
towels and hopped on icy
feet across gray linoleum
while outside in the dark
December night, wind howled
and ice coated the iron pump

handle.

Always lying in fresh, clean
underwear against fresh, clean
sheets in the ancient brass
bed at the top of the attic steps,
beneath hand-stitched quilts
that smelled vaguely of mothballs
and must and remembering the
migrant warmth of
the great tin tub.

BETRAYAL

They told me that my cougar was only a child's silly dream;
They told me so—and so—but I had seen
It purring/snarling in gray rocks that grew beyond the aspens
And had rushed back, faint from breath held in suspense
To warn them all. "Child," my grandmother said,
"There are no cougars here. They are all dead
Or hidden high above the snowline in caves. No alarms
Have rung for years down here, close by the farms."
                   And I believed.

They told me he would heal, that his red blood
Staining rusty flagstones would wash away, would flood
Away as soon as Grandpa sluiced the water
From the irrigation ditch across the lawn. It was hotter
In the kitchen late that night. Grandma stoked
The cast-iron stove, boiling water while they broke—
Or tried to break—his fever. Grandma made my bed
In the attic darkness. In the morning he was dead.
                   And I had believed.

They told me that the park was safe—that I could run
There on my way to meet my father as the sun
Sank red. I saw him coming—and from the brush
Head-high beside me, a German shepherd in a rush
Exploded. My father yelled—the dog fled
Yipping like a thing in agony. My father caught my red
Red blood in a paper soda-carton—irrational, insane—
But all I saw was redness and black pain.
             They said ... they said ... they said;
                 And I believed.

THE HOUSE WE OWNED

in the first house we owned we
painted plastered nakedness
rainbowed semigloss

shadeless bulbs cast black pterosaurs
out of heaven
onto semigloss plastered nakedness

night smelled odd
parents' murmurs in distant
rooms wrapped
stiff scent of paint
in familiarity

in bedrooms we would own we
rolled pillows next to naked
walls   huddled in blankets on naked
floors and in Montana
midnight
dreamed

auroras spackled stilldamp paint
through panes innocent of drapes
naked
to the night
naked to murmurs and strange smells
filtered through
the first house we owned.

SLEDDING IN MONTANA

the winter I turned twelve
Montana froze—
our southeastern square
a solitary igloo block
beneath ice-sheer
dawn

awake to sheeted grey
slate-silver stretched
sky to ground beyond
bedroom windows veiled
in frost—
empty fields behind suburban tracts

glittered tumbleweeds among
black posts
undressed by wire or slats
marking backyard lines—
erectile spoor on white
granite

when—wrapped nose-to-foot —
we ventured out
our arctic-empty backyards lay
glazed in contiguous ice
smooth as chilled
Montana winds

our sleds could course
uninterrupted
the entire block—

propelling northern blasts
caught

woolen coats
nylon parka hoods
knit scarves
black buckled boots
and sent us sliding sliding sliding
in long lyric glides
the length of a ten-house block

we did not know (then)

that just beneath
newly scarred ice lay frozen
excrement
expelled in darkness from bursting
hidden underground
septic tanks

Snow Draperies

Noon—at 20°—and the branches of leafless
elms across the road bend beneath
nine-inch-thick crisp lanes of
snow

piled flake by flake through four windless,
sunless, cheerless days—not star-flakes,
but frost-points piled on piles of
snow.

Twilight—at 3°—and the branches of leafless
elms across the road twine beneath
nine-inch-thick drapes of curving
snow

arced limb to limb, caught in the flagrant
act of melting by icy breath and frozen
in impossibly solid drapes of
snow

hung from branch to black branch, stark white
against Wasatch sky-pinks and winter-deep-
bright-blue sloped vertical mountain
snow.

An Act of Contrition

A roiling tumbleweed, propelled by west-
Blown gales, seems a kamikaze jest
Hurled by God across grey, fading snow,
A winter's-not-done-yet, intrusive pest.

It joins the other detritus below
My window—a tattered, cast-off Christmas bow;
A pizza box; remnants of a New
Year's bash—fossils from a week ago.

Windows roar like caged beasts in a zoo;
Tree limbs flail, hang drunkenly askew;
Ragged lawns lay barren, sere, and brown,
Parched for warmth, haggard in their rue.

And for the moment, winter's rancors crown,
Their savage features clenched into a frown.
It seems as if no joy, no sweet delight
Endures. I shrink beneath cold's leaden gown.

Then with a breath, all shifts: snowflakes alight,
First one, then ten, then multitudes in flight,
Welcome as a long-awaited guest,
As winter begs forgiveness, garbed in white.

Summer Stanzas

I roam summer paths—
Stanzas bud beneath my feet;
Words break into bloom.

I gaze across a pool—
Open shadows jewel cool banks;
Water lily cups
refract blue sky … secret souls
In polished petal tips.

Hidden pond-frogs sing—
Rippling strains of conscience frame
Voiceless summer rites.

Sunlight glints, flickers
Of flame ignite noontime breath;
Frozen firelight
Dilates hushed, blue-green spheres….
Dragonflies hover.

Swallows overhead—
White-cap-ripples gliding on
Calm crests of Memory.

Snails navigate
Jade-blades, float on willow-foam—
Paths lie hidden, though;
A snail has crossed my walkway.
Hours shift silently.

On butterfly wings,
Microscopic gem-scales speak
World-immensities—

How to Make Raspberry Syrup

First, rise early, while the first July
dew still washes the berries. Wear
long sleeves, long pants, even though
the air already bears the signature
of summer heat—otherwise long thorns
will scratch, not deeply but enough
to burn and itch. Wear thick-soled
shoes as well since often fallen
canes, dead and brown, can pierce
thin soles.   Pick at least a quart,
being careful to push away
thick pads of leaves and peer
inside, behind the canes in shadows
along the fence where the plumpest,
sweetest berries cluster as they
work on generating seeds. Be wary,
though, that none drop down
behind the canes to molder useless in
layers of last season's leaves.
                                        When
you have filled your pail (easier
to do if it has a bale to loop securely
over your arm) wash the berries
immediately in icy water, watching
minute beards, bits of leaves, the occasional
ant or spider skimming the surface.
Scoop the berries out by hand, noting
how they stain your fingertips
a rich plum-purple-red. Place

them in a pot. Mash them thoroughly
and sugar to taste (and note, too, how
the small white granules swirl
amid the throbbing pulp as you stir
to mix). Bring to a boil—remembering
the heat that is building up already
on shingles and eaves and leaves.
Set aside while you make fresh batter
from fresh whiteness: milk, flour,
soda, a touch of salt (of course,
the eggs will tinge the batter yellow.)
    Cook a plate-sized pancake
on the sizzling griddle, turning once
so both sides crisp brown.
Baptize thoroughly in rich
imperial sweetness, letting syrup
pool around the platter. Cut
the pancake neatly in bite-sized
squares and slide them one by one
through the syrup. Eat ...
Enjoy.

Melmac

The winds blew forty below
the night his package arrived,
brown cardboard masked
and taped.

They slit the packing, pulling out
and *ahhh*-ing each smooth
piece. Unbreakable. The latest
thing.

The oldest boy curled a saucer
in his smooth palm, spun it
against warped gray linoleum
and watched.

The saucer glanced across an arc,
skidding icily and swirling
like the snow beyond the glass,
and did not break.

Beneath, the toaster lay concealed.
They plugged it in. Houselights
dimmed a moment, then surged back
to strength.

They browned toast from frozen
loaves, served on flawless quarter-inch
Melmac, layered with honey and melted
butter.

That night, the four of them ate
toast from Melmac plates, four loaves
of white-bread toast from the freezer, and
thought of him.

Tornado Weather in Montana, 1959

Brittleness in light—
stark bright yellow
above circling dun bluffs—
stark blighting blackness in the west—
heavy electric air that stills
birdsong, and silences
July afternoon breeze.

Something—Coming—Soon—
scalp-itching, eye-twitching
weight of unnamable
Something—Soon—

And when it comes, relief
almost
before the terror of wind-fingers
hooking asphalt shingles,
of our frightened corner-huddle
with silent spiders
in the concrete basement

while the unseen-but-heard
funnel winds itself into a summer frenzy
not two blocks away—
dreadnought whine that blots
all other sounds along

the line of wood-shake homes
that shudder at its passing.
And
then

half-remembered
deafness as
it dies
and
drops
and

silver twilight blends the Rimrocks
surrounding Billings—
black slicks of water
studded with twisted branches like
ragged spears;
wheatfields snarled in good-morning
wisps of shattered gold;
windows broken, trees broken, power
lines broken into black bones
along the road—
and silver twilight
blends rain-black cliffs
with the passing breath
of Death.

1959

I.

In those Sputnik days when farmers' sons
mortgaged themselves for thirty years
to buy quarter-acre plots, turned plowshares
into gasoline mowers and, that done,
settled into eccentric complacency to sow
Kentucky bluegrass yards beneath manure loads—

In those prudish days we suburb brats knew
less of birds-and-bees than did our farm-bred
fathers, never having seen prize boars or Red
Rock roosters preening to their task. Clue-
less as to the precise mechanics, we waited taut-lipped
for the gutter-talk, the whispered slip

slyly advertent that proved *he* knew more than *I*,
or claimed to. We staggered in our innocence,
before the magazines and videos, uneasy with the assumed pretense
that *sex* would magically appear one day
and transform us into husbands, fathers,
without our having to pass some secret written test. Perhaps other

parents murmured to eager ears—mine did not.
So on that day, I was unprepared.
Sitting five rows back in Schraven's class, scared
to breathe, to move, staring at the flat
scarred desktop as if its convoluted scratches held
the key to sacred mysteries…praying to melt

into oblivion and take with me the creased
Levis suddenly (first time, all fevered flush

and blood-hot rush
without the blood, spared that at least)
as obvious as Cheop's pyramid. Ashamed,
not knowing why my body had betrayed me so, I heard my name

called out—Mrs. Schraven,
toad-like, squat-square,
short-cropped wrinkled cast-iron hair
and voice raven-
harsh ordered me to join the line beneath the grey-green
blackboard, and to recite…and to be seen.

II.

At recess, tight jeans sticky against my hairless legs and
hot asphalt shimmering mirages, making
yellow Four-Square lines shiver like desert sands,

I stood in an empty basketball key, slaking
chills with June heat, and watching as, across the yard,
surreptitious fights wove through breaking

lines of touch football teams. Knots of boys, already summer-hard
and rowdy, yelled as girls (still be-dressed and be-bowed back then)
clustered behind half-hidden giggles and stared

at arched backs and straining arms and muscled legs. When
Joey caught a hard straight pass, the girls squealed
as if to say they were not impressed by his orchestrated spin,

half-slip, and brave recovery. I watched from the basketball key,
alone as always in the vastness of the asphalt playground.
Still throbbing with my shame I did not see

Denny sweep around the corner of the brown
brick class-wing, running low and hunched, his hightops
slap-slap-slapping asphalt as he darted around

the volleyball courts, took four long steps
that brought him up beside me,
and as he flickered past clip

his fist into my crotch—on my knees
I gasped and swallowed hot mirages and saw
clots of ghostly girls and red-hazed lines of boys

pointing, laughing, and Denny—fist drawn
up in a victory salute, back to me as he disappeared
into the knot that was my class. Raw

shame blurred more than had the pain—
waves of sick-making pain I had not dreamed
my body could sustain

so long. Somewhere, far beyond the shocked-shell that seemed
all there was remaining of me, I dimly heard the class-bell ring.

We Built Forts

Sputnik was up. Grade school students saw *that* film:
Bleak in black-and-white, grainy pines contort,
Whipped by nuclear winds to manic palms,
Flaming heads to fervid ground   (*and we built forts.*);

A box-square tract home, two-stories solid,
Bends, bows, cracks, explodes its deafening retort,
Bequeathing nothing more than dust and squalid
Shreds…wicked tooth-pick shards   (*and we built forts.*);

Afterward, we bent young heads, crouched beneath
Soft-pine desks (engraved with scrawls of no import)
And—curled—prepared to stare Death in the teeth
Should fireballs appear   (*and we built forts*).

So we piled tumble-weeds as a last resort—
Six-foot walls of tumbled weeds…but we built forts.

They Had a Dream: 1959

That year was wet, with summer storms that blew
Thick moisture on the field behind
Their house. Tumbleweeds
Grew wild, tall and full, richly green
Until September's scorching breath
Transformed them into skeletons.

That fall, they built a house of tumbleweeds
Piled twelve feet high atop
A lath-and-wire packing box.
Inside, they cut out cardboard walls
And made two rooms where they could crawl,
Dried prickles crumbling down their necks
Whenever they disturbed
The shifting, makeshift roof

That day they played:
A father, mother, daughter, son,
An archetypal family,
Archetypal home beneath
The tumbleweeds, everything
As it should be for them to live
The lives their parents wanted them to have.

That evening when the father came
At twilight from his work, they took
Him out and showed what they had built.
He nodded, vaguely smiled
At the edifice of tumbleweeds
Stacked against the wire fence.
Then, "That's too dangerous," he said,

And made them stand across the alley-way.
He flicked a match.
It took one second for the dream to burn.

That was all

INTO BREAD

In the stone chapel (cold stone
where we would later bury
my grandparents) I sat, a
child among hard, chilling stones,

to touch communion with my
curling tongue and taste its sweet
dark life. Light draped smooth shadows
over hand-cut oak-plank pews

and cropped my fingers where they
curved the small glass cup…stained them
dark with life and caught a thin
white fleck of Christ upon my palm.

THE TRACTOR

We rode behind the tractor on the hay wagon—
Dirty, bare-chested, summer tans contending with dust
On knees and elbows. Cutoff-clad, we rode and whooped
And squinted when a sudden August breeze swirled
Chaff into our eyes.

We perched—three land-locked barnacles
On the tractor's steel-plate tire guards—
And stole slow, patient rides from alfalfa fields
A mile or more from home, the tractor's sun-hot
Metal baking blisters on our palms.

We jumped from the tractor's hitch and leaped across
Wide fields to secret fishing holes, while he—
Remembering another generation's boys and lines
And angular trout—jostled on alone to harvest
Knee-high stands of winter wheat.

We pulled the tractor upright with his mismatched team
And hard hemp ropes. We pulled the tractor upright
Where it toppled on March-frozen furrows.
We pulled the tractor upright and strained not to see
His blood…pale, mystic crystals on the twisted gearshift rod.

INTO THE FOREST

Into the forest, woods, copse (a word that
echoed eerily with *corpse* in my young
fears), grove, stand. Into draped darkness of mat-
ted needles, falcon leaves, where branches hung
with shadows shelter greens-to-black, where light
splays tricks and builds from nothingness threaten-
ing monsters *couchant*, where blue-violet,
purple-green hover just beyond lengthen-
ing day. Into the forest, where sun-heat
boils butterscotch from puzzle-pine bark
too hard to touch, where dawn-dew moulders wheat-
chaff dust to black, and moonlight stains wine-dark.
Into the forest, where colors blend art-
lessly into dark mystery at the heart.

Classical Music

haunts me even now—ghostly chords that reach
beyond three decades (almost four)
and pull me back. I hear again wild sounds that teach
my feet to dance on wooden floors,

my stockinged feet to dance on polished floors and swirl
and sway as if the universe
were me and I were it and nothing else—no world
no sky no sun no stars—rehearsed

in my uniquely isolated space. I danced
eyes closed, body liquid-sound
to flow into around and through a space entranced
by notes that none but I had found.

Fuchsias and Bleeding-Hearts—

remind me—inexplicably—of Elba
and the homestead...where such exotics
    could not survive the winters,
    could not endure without
Fruit-jar greenhouses perched on narrow
hand-cut ledges in windows rippled
with age.

And yet...they recall faint odors
of stale, earth-pack cellars clotted with remains
of summers dead, choked with harvests
set aside for winters yet to come.

They recall the five-foot, grey-white
wicker baskets arcing, fluted lip and twisted
handle, to tower over other vessels
at weddings...but more often at the funerals

that seem as well a solid part of Elba.
Fuchsias and bleeding-hearts droop in memory
    along the curves of Grandma's flagstones,
    along the lines of the cemetery on the hill—
but only there, in memory. In Elba,
such exotics could not, would not survive
the cold.

MONOLITH: THE TELLER AND THE TALE

SO Amy [*Aimee*, 'beloved', broke
Gramma's heart during WWII
being pig-headed, Dad once said]
           met us

by the hardpack driveway in
Monroe, Utah, one cloudless summery day
sometime back in
              '62

and before inviting us in—almost before
requisite kissin' and huggin'
country-kin-style was done—showed us
           the rock

AND traced a knobbly fingertip on grey
furrows she claimed told pictoglyphic tales:
A&E in Eden Indian-style but secret and
           sacred

and something she was blessed with,
dream-visions and interpretations of dreams, and
the trilobites in her ears dangled in
           shadows

from her jet-black hair, in shadows against
her dusky skin that pled dark blood.
Don't spread this around, she
           whispered

AS she segued into Hollow Earth and
Lost Ten Tribes before returning lodestone-like
to the flat black rock that told of
               Eden

[she said] and second-served as wheel-guard
warding wanton pickups from the fresh
and fragile green of her weedless
               garden

THE ROAD

The road, still roughly graveled, drops the length
Of a strong man's throw, angles down between
Hedgerows of sage and milkweed, even though
The houses on both sides are long since lost
To re-building and to disrepair. The road
Still travels furrow-straight past the homestead,
Widening slightly where tractors turned and turn
Into the yard. The house is no longer theirs,
Long since bricked over Grandpa's rough logs,
Cemented over Grandma's flowerbeds,
The wide boxelders cut and hauled away.

But the road continues straight, over the wooden
Trestle bridge where crawdads still prefer
Scrub-willow shades to sunlight flickering
On irrigation water brought from Cleveland's slopes.
The road runs straight to the first mile-post,
Then turns due west, between pastures still hip-high
Green, bordered in great mounds of golden
Wild roses, studded along the creek-banks with
Butter-irises in spring. It runs straight until
The northward turn at the city park, once little
More than weeds, now watered, mowed, waiting
For the next reunion to bloom with children's laughter.

From there, a mile to the north, then an angled turn
As sharp as Grandpa's plow lines, east this time,
Toward the rising sun and—one mile distant—
The final turn, and I stand again at the graveled
Drop, not having seen a single person

In the fields, a single child playing in overgrown
Front yards. A mile square, cut from the valley floor,
Where long years lost still huddle in cottonwood shades,
And memories bid me stay and rest in peace.

Her Journals

When she died, they found the box
Deep in the closet, beneath a stack
Of ancient sweaters set aside to darn,
A knotted skein of purple yarn
Half knitted into muffs, a rack
Of hats, some worn-out socks.

No one knew for sure what it
Might hold. No one had ever seen
It open. What treasures it might contain!
They found, first, a piece of plain
Muslin, thin, worn, but clean.
Beneath, what might have been bits

Of remnants—vivid colors bright
As new, hand-stitched in close designs.
And when they were unfolded: quilt tops!
Double Wedding Ring. Snow Drops.
Texas Star. Twilight Pines.
Drunkard's Path, scarlet on white.

Each piece…a memory of her years.
A bit of dress, or shirt, pajamas,
Aprons—each a frozen moment
In a web of loves well spent.
She'd penned no books, starred in no dramas;
These were the echoes of a life austere.

For My Son

I held him once in my single hand,
   Cradled a pod of soul
      A boneless breath that
         Would *become*
And watched pink furrows when he cried and
   Heard sweetness of laughter
      And tandem heartbeats
         As we slept;
Once I extended—fire beyond his
   Dreams—and formed illimits
      To amorphous worlds
         That he saw
And once I held him small and felt him
   Small and heard him small
      And wondered how he
         Could be large…

But now—

My father
   Frights me in mirrors
      Infests my thick fingers,
         Arms coarse with scars decades old and white
As shivered
   Ice in rock-choked beds
      Long dry. My children stare
         With lidded eyes (as I once watched him)
And I see
   My palms shoot his sleeves,

      My cheekbones slide beneath
            Young flesh—hear his wisdom speak to me,
Penetrate
   My fears to offer
      Rest and quietude.... And
          Now *he* holds *me* in his single hand.

CLAPBOARD MEMORY

We drove past my great-grandfather's place
Last weekend, on the way to the family
Reunion. I never knew him; he had died
Three years before my birth. I've seen him
In aging photographs, white-haired and stern,
Ice-eyes staring down, white mustache
Smooth as a melodrama villain's,
Although those who remember him assure
Me he was among the best-loved men
In the valley, open-hearted, generous,
Kind. He bought the place the year before
He died, never lived there full time; but
In the margins of the valley, it
Is still Sam Barker's place, six decades
Beyond his years. And the chicken coop
Still stands where he once stored the oaken
Table now centered in our kitchen.

The place is shaggy. Overgrown. No lawn,
Nor perhaps ever was, he being far
Too old. The roof sways. Windows stare
Glassless at the gravel road outside.
The porch sags, bringing weathered eves down
To drooping, sad half-smiles. Under clouds,
The shingles shrug as if to say, "Bring
On the storm, if you will; we've survived
This long, and will yet survive your floods."

We drove past. Did not stop. Barely slowed.
And when we reached the park where the

Reunion was to start, two old aunts sat,
Lonely, in the scanty shade of a
Rutted-trunked boxelder tree. Alone.

ANAMNESIS I

They've covered rough-cut logs with
yellow brick, the new people have; cut
down massive boxelder trees; planted
neutral grass where tulips, peonies, and
bleeding-hearts once flourished; replaced
white pickets with all-weather metal
mesh; removed the rusting hand-pump
by plank stairs. It's a different house now.

Nothing like the place I re-visit in
waking dreams, where half-a-century
ago a child gathered mottled eggs
from wooden nests; plucked plump
raspberries, eating perhaps more than
found their way into his battered
pail; trod an endless-seeming path
to an outhouse hidden well beneath
high-arcing cottonwoods;

where dwelt safety, warmth;
where questions left for years unanswered
rested, not yet asked; where every
moment locked in memory whispered
(whispers still, when I stop to listen)
"this is home, this is where you
ought to be."

I've lived in many houses since
those golden August afternoons, in many
towns large and small; grown used

to built-in bathrooms and electric
lights and concrete walls and smooth-
paved streets. But in my waking dreams
I recognize the place, the pull,
the power of this anamnesis to
calm, reassure, and restore.

Anamnesis II

Each time I stalk the valley's graveled road,
Pause near the creek that cuts the yard
In twisted ribbons only to explode
White fury beyond the bridge, I feel a shard
Of potent loss, as if my life had flowed
With passing currents, transformed to something hard
And brittle—long years become a pressing load,
Heavy with dead weight, dismaying, scarred.

It pains. Yet still I hearken to that place—
Green canopies of leaves where once I played,
Laughing echoes no murky age can churn—
Strong icons heartless time cannot erase.
All around, the past persists, decayed;
Each time I leave, I know I will return.

II. Today

Legacy II

and when She died her children slid
a hull a husk an
      emptiness
beneath black earth
where she was born
         and
stood in silent square
              one…two…many
    on either side
    at head
    at foot
        Daughter
        Son
        Daughter
        Son
            one…two…many

primitive rite
    Eden-old
submerging life in death
    hull in earth

no mourner grasped a mourner's hand

each
    stood
        as
            she
                had made them stand

  A
   L
    O
     N
      E

dependant on her chain
                                        her links
                 that held each bracelet charm
                      isolate
                      secure
charms   things   collected over years
                   one…two…many
      possessed
      treasured
for beauty they would bring her wrist
                         not theirs

they stood dependant one and one
and one and one
                     one…two…many

primitive rite of
      forgetting and
      forgiving and
      remembering

2

the old house   log and cement-mortar
roughhewn
        grey with age
                winter blasts
where she was born

bedroom transformed
through time to

    chicken coop
        hens
                one…two…many
protect
        enshell
            frail
                young
lest strangers steal
        [but they
        almost
        always
        do]
    in spite of beak
    and wing
    and spur

livingroom a washroom
        where the Maytag rests
        worn by bleach and time and
            decades of denim overalls
                one…two…many

behind   thick rows of raspberry
        canes
            crooked
thickets overgrown with weeds now
she is gone
        twig snakes twisting over
        broken irrigation rows
        twining through dry canes now
she is gone

3

"Where are all those people going?" she asks,
voice querulous with age and—truth to say—
with fear. "What town are we in now?" The *tisk-*

tisk-tisk (faint beneath freeway-roar) of paper
rattling in age spotted hands punctuates
fragility. "Where are all those people
going?" "What town are we in now? You
help me write names down on my map to see
where we are going." Pencil hovers, dips, swoops
wavering scrawl—unreadable—across
intricate contours on the L.A. map;
She hesitates, then speaks, more querulous:
"Where are all those people going anyway?"
she asks us again...*one...two...many....*

4
the End came slowly
        a g o n i z i n g l y slowly
                                it seemed

to those who watched and suffered
as She slipped
            through sleep
                       to silence

alone

although surrounded
        in her angular hospital bars
            by those she bore

standing in a square
            Daughter
            Son
            Daughter
            Son
                        one...two...many

prelude to her final breath
                        she had not
moved
      smiled
             spoken
                    wept
for five days
when at last
they
touched her cooling
                      flesh
and knew her
                    spirit
had escaped at last
whatever bounds its body
held

and

She

was

FREE

Afterward they walked
hand in hand
the solitary way that twined
through granite grass and dying clumps of blooms

                  one…two…many

one

Today

Today a radio talk-show host
excoriated Catholics and branded
infamous Mother Theresa for
condemning contraceptives
and questioned rabid callers about
one seventy-nine-year-old man's
retrograde absurdity
in the obvious face of
humanity's pressing need for a
million new and better ways to
prevent birth.

Today Reznikoff's Jews and Germans
conscience's Germans and Jews
marched in stolid single syllables across
the pages of Warsaw and Auswitz
and trailed Eichmann into Jerusalem and
stood naked/naked-making on broken
lips of man-made hells and shot/were-shot
(but how could those victims not be victims
to conscienceless destroyers of all things
that focused choice and fed responsibility)
and the Jews were shot were shot
again again again each time my eyes
dared another line of blood-black type
and crisp short unequivocal
words.

Today I stood sweating alone in the kitchen
my family being absent for a time
and washed apples from our backyard

tree, peeled them, cored them, sliced
them into three inches of steaming water
(as my grandmother had done, and
hers before), brought them to a soft
boil, spread just one cup of white sugar
and a sprinkle of cinnamon over the
froth that grew inside the twelve-quart
canning kettle and poured into boiled
clean mason jars with brand-new rings
and vacuum-sealing dome lids
white applesauce that
cost me not quite less to make at home
than if I had bought it in the store
(but that was the way my grandmother
had always made applesauce)
and I gladly paid the small small price.

Free Agency

Awake at half past six on Sunday morning—
The sky an arc of pale Lladro grey,
The air a shiver of December chill—

The children are asleep…my wife asleep,
And I should be asleep, since we stayed up
Till long past midnight, just the two of us.

But no—awake at half past six on Sunday,
The world is mine (except for two contentious
Cats outside my window, snarling and spitting).

All else is silence. I could read. I could
Walk. I could add the last few stitches to
The shirt I started sewing on last night.

Almost done, a blue-grey ghost upon
The cutting board, it waits. I should rise,
Walk a dozen steps, and finish it.

Instead, I find myself at my computer—
Its screen a sheet of pale Lladro grey,
Its whisper a shiver of December chill—

I could have sewn a shirt to wear today,
Or washed the china plates beside the sink;
Unwisely perhaps, I chose to write a poem.

Entire Unto Himself

Already cold and stiff by the time I arrived,
It was a shallow shadow, grey against black;
A collar of blood fringed its matted coat.

I picked it up, carefully, and placed it
Between plastic-shrouded seats, and then drove home.
A block away, light glowed through undraped windows.

The telephone sat silently. It had rung once that night;
A stranger's voice described the dog—where
To find it, what had happened…that it was dead.

That voice had sent me to the street. Now,
There was no voice, no echo, no sounds in the house—
No cadenced *clicks* of nails against linoleum.

I sagged into a chair. The family would return
Within the hour. The children would not notice,
Perhaps…but she would. She would know the loss.

I sat. Phantom weight pressed against
My feet where he had lain—that one place
Where he had not been wanted but that he chose.

Phantom breathing bled through stiff silences.
Finally, headlights pierced the windowpanes.
Her car pulled up the curving drive, and stopped.

I met her at the door, instead of him.
I whispered…something…words that held no sense.
And held her as she wept.

FATHER-CHILD

when my eldest rested long, strong fingers on my head and
prayed
in the shade of a white-washed patio
in the shade of hanging gardens watered by thin black plastic
conduits

it seemed
an oddity at first—a shivering clutch of tears—an emptiness
straining heart and gut
when
he said *Father*
and

I was unshaven, tousle-haired, dressed in dirt-stained pants
and a once-white T-shirt—eyes red with strain and chest
heaving with panicky breath and
he said *Father*
as if

he were speaking to God not me and he had never called me that
before
nor ever will (most likely) unless/*until*
he once again rests his hands upon my head to bespeak
my name
and title

HE IS NOT IN THE VALLEY

He is not in the valley,
Nor the valley in him,
But from each cut and curve
In I-15, parallel to the
Muddy irrigation ditch that
Coils along the foothills…,
Or over every flat of green
With tumbled hedgerows
Or weathered barns and stables
Propped, it seems, by blackened
Splintered fences…,
Even, once, in the wrist and
Hand, thick and reddened,
Of a stranger at McDonald's
Just north, in Richfield,
I saw/felt/heard him,
Nearly a century ago,
Playing in those same fields,
Treading through sage
On beaten paths that wound with
Swift irrigation ditches,
Watching wide-eyed
With his childhood eyes
His father's wrist and hand
(And his before) as they wrenched
Red-rust stubborn lugnuts from
A flattened tire, or smoothed
Sweet hand-cut plank to patch
Uneven steps or wobbling porch
Rails.
        So long ago.

Even the brick
Of homes, the mortar binding
Stone to stone, has crumbled,
And all that now remains—the
Homestead cabin alone
In flowerbeds behind
The white-board place
That bears his name still by its door—
And even so, I
See/hear/feel his breathing
Next to me,
His angled smile,
His jaunty whistle to
Accompany some tale of
People-places-things
I can never know…,
Yet recognize
In this narrow space/time/place
Between two mountain slopes.

Childless

Miscarry is a false name,
a misnomer (to commit more of the same)
that doubles back on me
and blames me for a clumsiness, a paradoxical need
to establish guilt even as I struggle to exonerate.

I *carried*—that much is true—up to a certain date,
some six weeks after our conception, I carried
a burgeoning egg married
to his absurdly energetic, patently pretentious sperm.
At nine months or so—what doctors call 'full term'—
I should have birthed and borne no more.

But they tell me I *miscarried*—as if exhausted by some mindless
　　chore
I merely stumbled, dropped my burden and, in error,
failed…as if I were a fantasy-Jill, struck in terror
by spilt well-water—
NO—but a Daughter,
a Son—a Child—that I would harbor, huddle

in my Self. By a subtle
and semantic shift, they whisper that all is for the best,
that had *I* not *miscarried*, I would be burdened, never blessed,
that he/she/it would certainly have come to breath *mis*-shapen…that I
should swallow pain like an aspirin, deny, and falsify
my *carrying*…should smile instead of cry

WHISPERS

Some words must be whispered after dark,
    When thirsty shadows drink all wayward sound,
        When whispers barely reach the porches
            Of thin lips…and cannot touch the sleeping ears
    Of those to whom they are said…cannot,
Will not enter a closed, unwilling edifice.

Some poems must be written in the silence
    Of deep midnight chill, with fingers cramped
        By cold, with mind and word-hoard stilled
        By ice that glaciers around the heart;
    Some poems would die beneath the heat
Of light and sound and easy sight.

Some loves must suffer innocent of life,
    Unspoken, dimly represented by a hand
        Twisting back a wispy hair, by turning up
        A quilt kicked-off some long time after night
    Passed softly into early morning, by unuttered words
That rise as tears, obscure an eye, and die upon a cheek.

BUD DIED

Today while I worried
about the leak in the roof
that has seeped rain water
into my daughter's room
for four worrisome years and stained
bits of her ceiling
urine-yellow

Bud died

Apples demanded to be
transformed
to sauce and jelly
strained
through tiny grids
of Tupperware and sealed
in squeaky Mason jars with lids
hermetically, conversely domed—
while I peeled and cored and pared

Bud died

I weeded on the hill
below the slump-stone fence
where the sun bears
down too strong and kills
most plants, but plumbago
and bougainvillea fare
better and have bloomed
sporadically since
April's torrents—

I weeded in their scanty shade lest they go
to weed as well and blue
blooms fade
to grey-white ghosts
dropping like doomed
spirits with the summer dew—
and as I thrust with my father's spade

Bud died

Now I whisper solace
to myself and forgiveness and understanding
because the roof is tight and
precise rows of applesauce
line the pantry shelf and
the hill is crowned in bright
colors to usher in
cool night

I Owe My Father Much

I owe my father much.

The shape of hands protruding from my sleeves—
Fingers coarser, blunter than my childhood own;

Forehead rounding high and arched beneath
Peninsular and fast-receding hair;

Echoes as I kneel beside my children's
Beds and speak my silence to their dreams;

Mirrors when I touch her cheek her hand,
Or rest beneath the fronding of her smile;

And music—an organist for forty years,
I play because he, softly voiceless, sang.

Behind deep shadows, where he sits to hold
A shadowed echo on his knee…

I owe my father much.

Alone, in the Chapel, at the Console

I find what I seek—
    In the not-quite-silence of the empty room,
        In the breathy rasp of air
Against metal pipes
    (Not-quite-music yet, not more than slip-of-air
        Over glossy edges of
Curving lips) I find
    Peace. Perhaps somewhere distant, beyond my sight
        And hearing, someone sweeps dust
From Sunday's carpet,
    Empties flecks of folded paper from trashcans
        Into larger, black-lined bins;
Or sisters defrost
    Armada refrigerators, preparing
        June's onslaught of receptions…
But I do not hear,
    Do not see, do not feel presences in my
        Dim sanctuary—I play
And, playing, speak with
    God in my own tongue—my hands, my feet conjoin
        To sweep me upward, away
To some unworded
    Place where sound lives pure, where silence dies, where ears
        Hear only wanted sounds, where
Tears—when they come—come
    Welcomed, wanted, embraced with all the lushness
        Of Garden dew, crystal Dawns

It's Hot and Sweaty Work

It's hot and sweaty work,
To make this monster speak
The way I want, to wrestle
With its stops and tabs
And pedals and keys, to
Bruise the silence with sounds
That—sometimes—match
Sounds inside of me…sometimes.

But mostly it's hot and sweaty.
Mostly my fingers slip from key
To key, fluid and flowing,
Like water rock to rock, glistening
And wild and out of control.
Sometimes my sweat mixes
With left-over hints of Sunday's
Bouquets and stings my eyes.

But mostly it's hot and sweaty.
It's work. I love it. I am alone
Then, alone with the monster
That has been part of me for
Almost four decades—alone
With the beast that can reduce
Me to tears, can lift me beyond
Words, can inflict greater agony
Than anyone outside of me
Can ever know.

But mostly it's hot and sweaty
Work.

Remembering the First Photograph of a Survivor

gaunt ravaged bareskull
taut
    cheek
        bones
flaying bareskin

hag conscience—black-on-
white
    hunger
        gnawing
fifty years unsated

grey on grey striped pajamas
hip
    bone
        bowl
inhuman nightmare

bonebloodbrain
rope
    thin
        sinews
binding bone to soul

JANUSARIES

WE breathe in separate hemi-
spheres
she
    and
                   I
not knowing when
backs turned
              irrevocably
    and
choruses of silence filed
miserly
between pursed lips
    and
tongues
        unraveled words
twisted over
           rivulets
      of mind
    and
silence ceased to speak
    and
        sounds filled
emptiness
with emptiness
    and
our separate hemi-
spheres
              split
with neither

quake nor sigh to warn us
of our

    dissolution

JUST TO SAY

thank you
to
the one

who laid a pair
of pruning
shears

open on
my driveway
yesterday;

I shall use
them
on the roses

and save
my four new
tires.

First Apricot

June always comes as a surprise.

May is bright-sand-bucket blue skies
And hermit buds crouched atop fresh-sap-green growth
Not there a week…a day ago.

May is hot silent air.
Temperatures crackling up to ninety—
The first heaviness in night-time air.

But June….

Here, June is gray-glow morning fog—
Coolness fingering through cool nights
Weeks after the furnace pilot-light has died.

June is breezes far too chill for summer,
Bud-blossoms slowing—color edging shyly from their furls
And tantalizing with clear promises.

June is hard green peaches the size of quarters,
Grapes like hard green teardrops
Knotted at the ends of yarn-vine clumps.

And one more thing—

June is one bright spot of red-flushed gold
Perched beneath a fan of leaves in the outward curve
Of an apricot branch—

Red-gold cheeks, mottled perhaps with purpled sun spots—
A spurt of sugared fleshiness
Caught in mid-flight between my teeth—
A sun-kiss hotly ripe upon my lips.

TULIPS

Memorial Day,
Elba, Idaho—1954

It's easy now to read about them—distanced
In time and place and mind through almost four
Long-dead centuries, when one brown, thin-
Wrapped bulb might buy a house, a ship, or more;

It's harder to remember a mere five
Decades back—swift breath to history—and
Wattled white cement twining along pine
Planks an equal breadth above moist brown sand;

And perfect tulips one by one, nodding
Staid humility to God—gaudy splashes,
Golden, purple, blood-streaked or pied, adding
Heat and flame to sunlight's vibrant slashes…,

Waiting all, for lopping—proud errant knaves—
And final rest upon our fathers' graves.

Cleaning the Garage

An evanescent spider filigrees
barren stucco walls
to crumbling concrete footings—

laces twelve-year-faded apricots
crammed curved-shell-up
in cloud-crazed mayonnaise jars—

laces water-clotted Clorox bottles that
disintegrate and with
*Small Bang*s flood the fruit room—

laces Great-Grandpa's bentwood bucksaw,
black elm-dust plaque
caked along dull rust-red teeth—

laces inch-thick dusty memories
and musted shades
of death and change—

APRICOTS THIS YEAR

And Plums. Apples, even, on the tree
That last year bore but ravaged
Fruit. The heat has not struck yet,

To turn dusted leaves to shriveled
Twists, to score deep velvet flesh with knots
And burn the Apricots before they blush.

WIND AND STONE

I am stone
enclosed by wind.

We share damp shores.
We hear black
waves break on
charcoal knots
that stud bleak shells
of rotted logs.

We breathe the breath
of pines that sway
urgent needles
sunward, earthward—
elegant arcs
ride surrounding winds.

We taste the trail
of water on air.
We smell and taste
and touch—river
and cove ripe
with wild strawberry.

You lean into the wind,
stroke its smoothness
into glass, release,
evaporate,
and supple-shape again.
You are wind.

You touch and warm
and move with subtlety
into thin crevices,
too thin to see.
You penetrate
dark hollow hearts

of stone

Making Love at Midnight

while two rooms away
children thinking themselves grownups
crouch on sagging sofas
in the TV room,

we search a sudden
darkness—fingertips long used
to touch of flesh
refresh vague memories of

newlyweds, when darkness, children,
television—nothing interfered. We
reach, and find the missing smoothness
disguised beneath a subtle sense of apricot

and passion flower and
roses blending essences against
a humid July darkness,
breathing outward their perfumes.

Distantly a lyric, haunting
lute adds substance to
the night, fingering our
ears with softness as

we each consume with
fingertip and tongue and
palm and lip. Years
retire. Lines of flesh

grow smooth and taut,
young again and virginal.

Only the slight sense
of apricot and rose

and passion flower separates
the touching, part to part
and whole to whole.
Twenty years ago, such

oneness was not yet
possible. Now—wordless—understandings
slip from one to
one, deeper than the

rhythms and the passions
and the necessary heat
that outstrips July night,
sears us into sleep.

THE PIGEON WOMAN IN COOLEY PARK

1.
flutter-whirr
      whirr-coo coo and
the pigeon woman in Cooley Park
skirts flustered in a March wind march-
es headdown shoulderbent body
bent
    against flat wind and around
                                her head
flutter-whirr   whirr-coo   angel
dusts of white and grey swirl
    whirl
        curl
cloudbanks drifting as she
                      drifts
the solitary path between
    two stands of oaks

Bare oaks.
The pigeon woman does not see
    does not listen
    does not speak
beyond a murmured
        coo coo my lovelies
        coo coo whirr
buzzing her tongue and
speaking with the pigeons
        that are hers

2.
Bread crumbs collect in dark pockets
stale with crusts and gritty with stray

sesame seeds tumbled loose and seeking
in the darkness for a spot of soil in which
to germinate and grow.

3.
The park is closed from sundown to
sunup, by *fiat* of the city ordinance
carefully spelled out in red letters
on the white metal sign hung
like a badge of office above
the concrete arch between
two squat pillars that hold
the wrought iron gates
that segregate
Cooley Park
at night.

4.
Pigeons wheel in tight
formations over grey pools
clotted with spring weeds

5.
There was
a child
once

         one

more years
ago than
there are
pigeons on

bare branches
in two
oak groves
along a
solitary

path

6.
The pigeon woman in Cooley Park
spreads dark hands and dribbles small round
yellow seed onto black pavement.

A woman in a bright green nylon
parka wheels her two-hundred-dollar
carriage past.

The pigeon woman does not look up.
The pigeons do not stir from their feeding.
The child does not cry as he is wheeled by.

The woman in the bright green nylon
parka sees the pigeon woman but does
not see her hear her listen to her care.

7.
Home is a shallow space
scraped beneath an overpass.
Cars hurtle over her head
without knowing she is
there, curled against herself.

She does not sleep. The pigeon
woman stares unblinking against
darkness, not listening to
the stir of cars over her head
and sees only darkness until

the sky lightens. She unfolds
her thick self, pulls a thick black
cloth coat tighter around her
middle and cinches it with a bit
of rope she found along the road.

She stands beneath the overpass,
a runner at her mark, until the edge
of the sun clears the trees
of Cooley Park, a mile distant
to the east. She stares at it and

does not blink until the sun
is round and low and ready.
Then she blinks, and the tears
form but are not wept.
There was a child once.

8.
The man is waiting for her
    behind the shop.
She has never read the sign over
            his brick red door.
She has never spoken to him.

He is waiting and holds out his hand
and she takes the small paper bag
    with its folded top
    with its creased sides
    with its rounded bottom
that holds

bird seed enough for a week
there will be no more
            [*she knows*
             but does not say]
so she must be careful.
Otherwise the birds
        must go hungry

She takes the bag and
the man steps inside the brick-red door and
he closes it quietly and

she walks on.

Cooley Park is half a mile away.
There was once a child.
She does not speak.

9.
Pigeons cut the sun—
Shadow-wings sever light from
Light at first dew-dawn.

10.
At sunrise, someone unlocks
the lock on the gate
between squat concrete pillars
                          and
the pigeon woman shuffles
through on her way
to the solitary path
between
          two
stands of oaks still
naked but beginning to bud
in March.

11.
At noon   the Processional moves
a crippled millipede through
Cooley Park

bearing banners and green bunting
shouting Wo/Men   bear
witness to Inequality

Intolerance
Incapacity.

Blue-jacketed troopers line
the cobbled path between
two stands of naked

oak   but noOne intrudes
argues shoutsback
throws offal at the

men walking hand/IN\hand   the
women\FOR/abortion   the
laughingChildren waving

gigantic LOLLIPOPS   screaming against
WarHomelessnessBIGBusinessOil
ObscenityBigotryNukes   and

noOne shouts back and noOne stalls
the forward flow of the eccentric
millipede to

speak to the pigeon woman   where she
sits back-toward-the-walkway hunched
over lifeless feathers

and a split of rusty blood
The Processional juggernaut rolls
over her   over the corpse of a dead bird

12.
When a child
dared to smile
     [*there was a child once*]
at the pigeon
woman later that
day—
 when the
 sun was leaning

      westward and deep
      shadows laced through
      naked branches—

                                               [*once*]

                a
startled mother jerked
a small arm
and whirled a
small body sideways
and marched away

13.
noOne noticed except the
pigeons
     mindless fluffs
of feathers
without brains
to speak of
without memory
without understanding
with only instinct
and an emptiness
in bellies without
seed
noOne thought to check the recesses of the hollow
beneath the overpass a mile from Cooley Park
After a while
the pigeons no longer
congregated in the
naked branches
of the naked oaks
beside a path.

14.
Once there was a pigeon woman in Cooley Park

BANK OF VIRGINS!

That's what he said, I swear,
that's what he said
right there
on channel five, prime time,
some faceless mouth
huckstering between
two episodes in an endless flow
of clatter:
        "Bank of Virgins!"
I almost cracked my neck
snapping to attention, urging
traitor ears
(that so often fail
to hear
what is truly said) this time to slow
the patent chatter
and concentrate on syllable
and word: "Bank of Virgins!"
Unspeakable, unprintable
conjurations flooded me—
Would one wish to
deposit or withdraw? pay fees
for services? or merely charge and owe—
sexual shop now, pay later.
        Once more, I thought, and watched
his thin lips frame
the phrase—and caught
my error (simple enough). As I
heard "Bank of Virgins!"
and let my wild perversions fly,
another mundane "Van conversions!" echoed
from the TV trader.

Shipwrecked Among the Channel Islands
Suggested by a line by Judson Jerome

Cast up with just their jock
straps and their knives, the
Torrey Beach men's baseball
team infests the island—so
many scuttling crablike bodies
quarreling over freshets, over
heaps of unripe oranges that
might or might not stave off
starvation for a month.
        Back home in Torrey Beach
one was a grocer, one a
dentist, one an assistant to
the high school dean of boys.
Another peddled life insurance door
to door. And yet another daubed
paint on stretched-out canvases and
tried to sell the end results at the
local Sunday swap-meets.
        But here, cast up with just
their jock straps and their
knives, alone, it's hard to tell
which one was which. Blood
swirls in darkened patches on the
sand; blood whorls in twining
patterns on smooth rocks. Knives
wail as blades insinuate between
thick ribs. Waves pile sand on
sand, hide hollowed orange rinds;

and freshets flow with saltiness
more primitive than primordial
ocean swells.

RITUAL

we stare he and I strangers faceless voiceless bound
by common nature's need   we stare at grout ground

ruthlessly between white tiles   we stare as if the world
were captive in grey porous squares   we swirl

in streams unwanted pungency acrid   fools' gold
flashing lightning sallow on white to fold

moist patterns silver-throated swallowing   hide
brotherhood in coldly grouted stares   tide

slackened staring mindless motion disconnected
separate   ritual assumed   ritual enacted

Sparks

Tin-
derdry—
sparks flick poems

my
way—ig-
nite dead leaves

Theys
touchlife
awefully—touchlife

touch
voiceflesh—
touch dreamseas

crys-
talshattering
dreamseas—touch

turn
transform trans-
mute leadgold

poems
into
livingflesh

and
nubs rub
nipplebright

thru
convolu–
tions braincrackling

electric-
al lightshows
sexual almost

Theys
speak one ruby
rose—speak foreign

death
and
alter rivermind's

flow
and touch
and touch

and spark
newfires
smouldering before

be-
neath deadleaves
and blackrot soil

I, Homeless

Homeless I sit, patient, at the corner.
Cars flow past, return, and flow again.

Roofless, I sing my lullabies beneath
sharp shade of palm fronds that cut
harsh light into thin strips that sizzle
on white concrete beneath a summer sun.
    Homeless I sit, patient, at my corner.
    Cars flow past, return, and flow again.

Windowless, I watch their world. Through plaited
drapes of smog I watch their leather shoes,
their pleated cuffs, their second-skin-tight hosiery
as walkers skirt by me so carefully unseeing.
    Homeless I sit, patient, at my corner.
    Cars flow past, return, and flow again.

Roomless, I feed my daughter beneath our
kitchen-shrub, brush leaflets from her shoulders
as she draws life through a bent McDonald's straw
and rattles remnant ice in her paper cup
    Homeless I sit, patient, at my corner.
    Cars flow past, return, and flow again.

Roomless, I turn my back to the constant flow and let
tired eyes slant shut—not quite, but enough
to rest and still watch out for her. I hope
for ease…I dream of roofs and once-white walls.
    Homeless I sit, patient, at my corner.
    Cars flow past, return, and flow again.
    Flow past, return, and flow and flow again.

Damon Again

Milton felt no frost when Damon died,
No chill eclipsed the hot Italian sun
Or touched his neck and drew an icy line
Into his heart—he did not know the pulse
Had softly stilled, the breath, the voice, the mind.

> *If we dwelt in Arcadia,*
> *His flocks would weep with mine*

Nor I, working in my roses, cutting
Canker from thorny limbs, twisting back
An errant branch and twining it again
Where it belonged—heat poured its June in May
And I worked silently, unaware.

> *If we dwelt in Arcadia,*
> *His flocks would weep with mine*

Five decades now—and we have drawn upon
Each other time and again for strength, for joy,
In sorrow, in pain—five decades … and still,
As if standing alone, I did not feel
You pass. I should have.

> *If we dwelt in Arcadia,*
> *His flocks would weep with mine*

I should have felt earth shake, air weep, fire chill
To ash, water freeze to solid—all
Infinites at once time-bounded, space-
Constrained. And did not. It took a phone call
From your son for me to know.

If we dwelt in Arcadia,
His flocks would weep with mine

But we do not.
And thus, farewell.

After Thirty Years of Teaching

Then, at ten, (younger and smaller than all
The others) I sat quietly at my
Wooden desk, already shy, watching fall
Transform into snow as a darkened sky
Lowered, and classroom lights in room and hall
Glowed, making her room a still, shadowed sigh
Except where violets consumed the pall,
Breathed purple gleams for students to dream by.

Then, all I wanted was to be like her:
To teach—no matter what, no matter who—
And fill *my* student's minds with flowering
Violets, to shatter winter's hold, spur
Thought to leafy thought, until something *new*
Burst forth, immaculate and towering.

PORTRAIT OF THE ARTIST ON THE VERGE OF MIDDLE AGE

On the raw canvas of words, images form;
Superimpositions blur
Boundaries—

Strangers' hands, scarred and
Blunted, creep along…
My father's

Hands, not mine—no graceful, long
Musician's fingers; instead,
Short blocky

Farmer's hands that knew the plow,
The pump, the sawblades scraping
Knuckles broad

And soon arthritic. On the raw canvas
Of words lie painful blueprint
Planes of face

That soon will be my sons; glint of eyes that
(Darker brown) gleam when my
Daughters smile.

Double-, triple-, quad- and
Quint-exposures—aging
Photographs

Curl, some faded black and white…and
Superpose my past upon a stranger's
History.

For Grace Isabella

The Crown Without the Conflict
14 May 2003

I saw you once…and last,
As I wrapped you in white
And laid you beside your toys…
Teddy Bear, Bunny, Locket,
Recording of your father's
Voice that you had never heard.

I saw you then…counted
Toes and fingers, saw the tip
Of a tiny nose, as much
Intuited as saw eyelids in
Sleep. Not much more….
The hygromas (ugly word,
Uglier in life than in the
Read) and the hydrops
Blanketed all else in their
Insatiable greed to
Absorb fluids, tissues.

Still, I saw you…in the arc
Of nose, the slit of
Eyelids, the curve of
Spine against the sheet
The hospital had wrapped
You in. And it sufficed.

You remain part of my son
And of his love
And of his parents
And of hers throughout

Long links and chains
Of genes and cells
And Spirit throughout
Time.

QUILTING

Piece by piece I deconstruct my
quilt, tugging threads frayed and
worn by unsped years, teasing
knots once-taut-now-tense until they
ease and patterns once-unthinking-clear
blur and fade and

piece by piece my quilting deconstructs
itself and tears a life to puzzle-
patterns patchwork-crazy hazy
reminiscences of vivid childhood
shirts and cowboy PJs and dresses that
she wore and tore and

piece by piece constructed quilted
stitched patterned after the imagination
of her world and wrapped us cotton-
batting-white-and-firm until
we could not move but slept and
dreamed and seemed and

piece by piece surrendered rendered
deconstructed to her construction and
accepted quilting as our own and bore
the prickled nettled thumbflesh-prints
of needles weaving intercessantly that
made and frayed and made again

piece by piece their mute coherence
dominate regulate militate until
—almost to late—bleached backing
wore too thin, lining showed, and

pattern separated deconstruction and I
could rue my see-through quilt.

I HAVE TIME

I have Time too much, too much—
It plods in soft amœboid rounds,
And mutes all loftier echoed sounds,
Transposing solid to velvet touch;

I have Time too slow, too slow—
It varies with each hour, each day,
And mocks the leaden, measured sway,
Confusing clock and engine's flow;

I have Time, an artful fraud—
Instructing me in death and fear—
That makes me yearn anew to hear
The eternal metronomic Time of God

III. Memory of Applebuds

I Have Seen The Mountain

I have seen the mountain glazed with
      shooting stars and
      violet petals curled beneath a too-near sun;
I have seen the mountain bristled with lodgepoles and
      spruce, blue-green tufts hiding
      blue-grey sky and falling dry to
      carpet bone-rich earth.
I have seen the mountain meadowed with
      the vivid chest-high green of water hemlock,
      broad embroidered leaves,
      thick stalks,
      thick finger-roots to dig into saturated soil and
      store convulsions, spasms, death.

I have heard the mountain whisper hot secrets distilled through
      butterscotch Ponderosas and boiled from
      manzanita in the summer sun.
I have heard the mountain speak in heavy drops of summer rain
      striking stretched canvas roof and walls and
      cooling sin-fine dust that
      clots the trails and
      clots the throat and
      clots the mind.
I have heard the mountain wrench in warning
      when black thunderheads hung crucified
      on granite spikes
      and wept wet pain in avalanching
      rust-red river-blood
      and cursed wet pain with crooks of
      lightning blasting granite into knives

        blasting tree crests into embers
        blasting solitude

I have stood upon the mountain naked
        to pinwheeling stars and felt warm
        night winds touch me with revelation
I have searched the mountain through its hidden washes
        crouched back to stone in narrow chimneys
        gripping living stone with living flesh
        to urge my body upward
        one more foot
        one inch
I have sought the mountain from its barren summit
        above the faded fringe of stunted lupine
        above the twisted limbs of stunted pine
        above the rings of ranges stretching outward
        infinitely
        lower, greyer, lesser—
    knowing
        that there is no more to seek

I have knelt upon the mountain and tasted
        its stony
              silent
                      heart

MORNING BELLS

Imagination invites me to hear
Dim morning bells—slight slate-blue turbulence
Against an opaque yellow-cream sky. There,
Where night and day, blue and sable, balance
To ward dawn—in that instant, that moment
Of unraveled Time, I hear Morning Bells.
Jasmine-sweet they crochet sound and segment
Sight, construct daylight with an audible
Rise and flow, rhythmic ebb and fall. They seal
Irrevocable boundaries, divide
Little-Death from Life, impel blood in pale
Arabesques, and cool arterial flights
Of unbreathed crispness, unseen vapor trails—
    Elegant subtleties of Morning Bells.

APPLEBUDS ASSAULT SLICK PEWTER MIST

Applebuds assault slick pewter mist
With throbbing promises—
Protuberant, they leap from limb-knots warmed
At dawn

To petal brightness through corolla-nests
Of dusky green. They mass
In rose-throat armies redolent of thick
Perfumes

And bend rough branches to their weight. They
Flare, advance…retreat—
In haste they cast aside worn, pale disguises…
White robes

That covered richnesses and soon, their tasks
Fulfilled, drop uniform away—
To leave flush memories of applebuds
Long gone.

Morning Glories

Banked Morning Glories robe our weathered fence:
Regal purples, sky-foam blues, pinks as deep
As childhood smiles, and clear soul-white. As dense
As years, blooms pile on secret, midnight greens
At dawn. They wake, unfold thin tissue wings
To drink sweet light. Before we rise to play
Fond childish games, they make shamed morning sing
Its brightness brighter, lest their glories fray
The sun's. At noon they hover—birds beyond
A shadowed stream so deeply green it seems
To pulse with inner light. They harbor sounds—
Bee-songs, insect-hymns. They tendril between
Pale moments. Then Morning Glories calmly
Furl soft velvet-silk when grey evening calls.

CHOOSING IRISES

Picking iris on a day
      Sometime in spring
      Somewhere north and east
Of Sacramento—

It must have been late spring,
      With blue-bowl sky,
      Cloudless lest a hint of shadow
Mute colors—

Up and down the rows,
      Drinking fragrance,
      Feasting of violets,
Amethyst, white, powder-blue

At two-bits a start come fall
And dividing time.

We got the call that late
      September, drove—the two
      Of us—therewhere
In her old, faded Chevy;

The owner met us with three bags—
      Brown sacks stuffed full
      Of broken rhizomes webbed
With whiskered roots,

Crowned with remnant nubs
      Of spear-leaves dried to husks,
      Curled around white knots.
They seemed dead.

He promised:
"Wait 'til bloomtime comes."

When it came—a winter passed
    With trudging steps,
        And sea-froth tips transformed
To leaf and bud—

We stepped out each by other,
    Day into day,
        Until they
Burst

Grape-heady snow six-inches wide,
    Red-almost-black that bled
        On too rough palms, butter
Crowning three-foot stems—

And I remember, with the iris,
A promise: *"Wait 'til bloomtime comes."*

BARTLETT PEARS

do not ripen on the tree but wait
hardgreen the killing kiss of frost
to tum-

ble into dark and quiet places where
their secret chemistry works from crisp
core out-

ward yellowing and ripening until taut
surfaces soften and stems turn black
and spill-

ing fragrance announces harvest-home.
Spring Bartletts sway in white-green buds
and blos-

soms and turn stiff backs into stale winds
but August Bartletts hide beneath
soon fall-

ing leaves and scorn to show their greenness
to long-waiting eyes. September Bartletts tease
with hints.

Beyond the Harvest

Late-set apples half-grown wither
in grey chill among grey remnant leaves
splotched with cankerous yellow and
green. In solemn clusters, pendant

almost-apples counterfeit red rinds
brushed with subtle streaks of deeper
dusty red. Huddled above jutting, naked
lower branches, hanging isolated

to January ice, they parody saucy
swell and ripe roundness of September,
tease distant eyes with prospects
unfulfilled. Tomorrow they will lie

beneath black layers of wind-strewn
leaves…softening, sagging inward,
disintegrating…to become their own
full-blossomed progeny in warmer days.

Restoration

November wind—and ice behind the promises—
ragged clouds pulled thin—Asian pear dipped
leaf-first in mustard, dried soot-black bark—
roses curled fœtally furl in furls, red stained
dark—iris crisped, melting bonelessly—and

sharpened pencils nudge swollen bases,
emerge point-most over blood-brown
bark—sheath-wrapped veins urge up and
out and November winds swirl promises—

Cymbidium budstalks break winter silence

Cambria Shoreline

CAMBRIA, CALIFORNIA

                I

God not yet
finished
blending green to grey
    turquoise to magenta
    silver to the flat dull sheen of lead
wrinkles

a sodden black tarp upon
the shelf jutting at Cambria
and spills

green algae
    blue kelp
        white froth
drop
by
drop

                II

Straight ahead, the ocean shines
in flat-edged silver shingles, while

left, it merges dusky green
with shadow-haunted ghost-seals

and right—north—it shades to grey,
molten lead as deep as agate.

III

I will pretend that the rock out there
swirled in foam
rises and falls in a stable sea

thrusts and breasts and thrusts
to rise
beyond the low imagination

Breakers form — I will
pretend
canting shadows flicked

from an afternoon sun will
rise and fall — a
sea lion perhaps or merely seal

capturing a quick ride into
oblivion
on behemoth's floundering back

The Irrigation Ditch Lies Dead

The irrigation ditch lies dead,
Strangled by a web of pipes—
Cold concrete. It fed
The upper pasture once, then tumbled

Through knots of milkweed whisper-white,
Past apple orchards to thirsting gardens;
Along its way it glistened light,
Mysterious and subtly green.

It welcomed naked feet; it called
To dusty flesh on August days;
It steamed in crisp-cold mornings, walled
Itself in ice when winter dropped—

And now lies dead. The milkweed, wilted,
Wings no frothy seed. Orchards
Pant in heat. The gardens—jilted—
Await in vain their concrete lover's flow.

NESTLING

I

They hatched today. Last night
when I peeked among the apples
they were eggs, four, end to end
among twigs and scraps and a twitch
of white yarn looped up and around,
an inadvertent infinity.

> *Jamie called*
> *last night to say he was doing well*
> *and for her not to worry.*

This afternoon I stood on tiptoes
at the patio's edge and saw her tail
upright, white striped with charcoal gray,
upright and alert. I backed away and
moved to the other side of the concrete
slab to finish the barbeque.

> *Jamie was going to come by for dinner*
> *but did not. His mother thinks his car*
> *broke down again, but I don't think*
> *that was the reason.*

After dinner, while we were cleaning up,
I glanced at the nest once more. She was
perched above my head on the power line,
and this time when I leaned into the apples
she shrilled at me—and then I saw four tiny
bits of greyish fluff, four sharp orange throats
stretched taut and expectant. It startled me.
She shrilled again, and I stepped back
into the shade.

> *Tonight Jamie called but would*
> *not speak to me. His mother cried. I waited*

> *but he would not speak through*
> *the static and the silence of*
> *the telephone.*

Sitting in my office, I can hear them, a subtle
chirrup just beneath the Mozart horn concerto
playing on the tape to ward away the silence
and the memories.
Their infant song hangs softly
fragile on the air, underneath the mellow horns.
I shall leave the window open for a moment more,
then slide it shut, shut out their nascent song.

II

One died.

An unripe apple
slid
too soon
onto the rumpled
nest
> *One died.*

Hollow bone and
hollow almost-pinfeathers and
empty skin
jumbled
in black twigs and
white twine.
> *One died.*

Eyeless
sockets black
above a withered beak
crumpled like a bit
of yellowed
ivory
> *One died.*

Small black ants
trail

down
the trunk   disappear
beneath shaded umbels of
dill

III

The other three are gone

Morning brought the adults
with the dawn   they echoed through
leaves hung heavy with green
apples   they flicked greyandwhiteandgrey
through shadows

The other three were gone

The nest slid sharply groundward
its outer lip torn   twigs pulling away
as if too grownup to be held in
precious tension with the rest

The other three were gone

cat perhaps   or 'possum from across
the road   or fruitrats from the plums
beyond the fence
no feathers marred the white rocks
beneath the tree

But the other three were gone

At night   when heat presses against
dull windows I hear them   high pitched
demanding   throatstretched and
waiting   tomorrow I will take out shears
and cut the nest away before the apples
ripen

IV

Jamie called
from Baltimore—a continent

away from
us. He arrived safely, he said,

and hoped to
find work soon. He spoke ten minutes

with her, less
than thirty seconds with me—"Hi, Dad,"

followed by
naked silences and long breaths

that spoke most
eloquently of long-dead words

ice angers
raw retreats. Slick static on the

line sounded
high and thin—nestlings' hungry cries—

and both of
us breathed unspoken promises

to brace bare
branches and mend an empty nest

Off-Shore Flow

grey grey cataclysmic
       gradient
clouds
   barricade
grey coast
      from
             grey
choked valley
    burned
    grey

JuneJulyAugust withered
   sunbland
     grey

flat
tepid
distilled
      and
            tasteless

summer

The Tyranny of Equilibrium

Along this stretch of beach cold sands sing
subharmonic counterpoint to the rushing wings
of gulls.
                The day is clouded—gun-metal gray
from land to sea. Waves curl
like mercury—heavy, glinting in the lulls
between ebb and surge
and inching on the breasts of weathered dunes.
                Beyond the cove I cross a point
of blackened rock hung with shaggy green
that floats like dead men's hair from blunted
bones. The keening wind holds the gulls static now.
                Midway between tide and cliff
a bleached palm heart rocks
feathered, salt-stiff
fronds against a whitened core
that mocks bones, and seems a beached
and desiccated plesiosaur,
some half-forgotten Nessie
dying in the mercury sea.
                I walk the length, south to the final spit
of toothless boulders.
I stand and stare, then sit
for longer moments than I planned
on damp unyielding sand
before I retrace my footsteps.
My feet are blackened by bits
of tar—they will stick uncomfortably
to my shoes as I drive away.
                It is noon.

The wind is colder,
and the cold sands are
silent.

WALNUT HARVEST
1958-1962

Come fall, we'd gather with the rest,
Mostly relatives, a few kids from
The neighborhood, to glean the best

Fresh nuts, fresh fallen, rattle-hollow
In stiff, curling, blackened hulls.
Long sacks dragging, we would follow

Leo on the tractor, Bessie with the kids,
And mound our shaggy piles of nuts,
Checking carefully for the last few hid

Beneath thick tufts of sports that sprouted
From black grafted trunks. Bags full,
We dumped our harvest in the bin, routed

Hull-encrusted nuts through brush
And water baths that scrubbed them clean
And dripped wide muddy palettes to rush

Beneath our feet as we, shoulders sun-burned
Wrists cramped, fingers stained deep walnut-black
For days, clutched our precious nickels painfully earned.

WEEDING IN THE POETRY BEDS

Weeding in the poetry beds…pottering
Among rank lines and wayward words
That beg for pruning pens…tottering

On the edge of fertilizing (for the third
Yet futile time) that haiku planted years
Ago, the one whose structure looks like bird

Claws as it crooks across the page to rear
Its capitals at me and dare
My worst—weeding in the beds I shear

Lopsided growths from sonnets, pare
Thick rinds from villanelles, stir the roots
Of free-verse vines that grudgingly share

Pages with rigid triolets. Some shoots
Demand more patient care. I prop
Their failing stresses, tamp with heedful boot

Damp soil around decaying quatrain-crops
In hopes that rich, dark humus might revive
Slow, flagging growth. I shape slick tops

Of thick-leaved dactyls hedging lively,
Hiding rough brick garden walls.
I wait. Some words may die, some survive

Parching summers and frosting falls—
Some will surmount my cottering
Fresh word to word, will bud and blossom tall.

MATRIX, BY MICHAEL R. COLLINGS * 157

CONTINUITY

The river passes, gurgling its thoughts
beneath the level of my comprehension.
I think I know the spot, the shore, the awkward twist of branch
on the dead oak just across the glimmer—
I feel I know the spot, the shadow,
the whitened air cascading with small puffs from cottonwoods.

It seems familiar—and yet I know that while all else
seems familiar, while the river passes
unimpeded, uninterrupted,
I see it for the first time
and the last
precisely thus—as molecules from far distant
foreignnesses slip by—
infinitude of molecules I have never greeted,
never known, never seen
and never will—
and yet it seems I think I know the spot.

The twist of oak is not the same.
A flake of drying bark has shivered from its branch.
A sparrow snapped a single twig
to help construct a nest, perhaps, since last
I stood by this small stone, itself
transformed by grit swept past.
One dangling leaf surviving from its green-time
might have tumbled to the earth to hide itself
in humus thick below.
And so, the twist is not the same,
and yet it seems I know that branch.

And the air, rife with cotton just as last time,
yet not the same, not just, but altered with each second
each breath of mine and wind that whirls
across the river's dimpled whorls.
Not just the same
and yet it seems I know the air,
have breathed this air and watched this air
before.

And so it goes. All changes. All remains
unalterably the same, perhaps, within the tumult
of imagination. And somewhere, trapped beneath
familiarity and essential foreign-ness,
between what seems and is,
the river *is* the same, the oak endures,
the flagrant tufts of aging white
have been and are and will remain and
I think I know this spot and do.

IV. The Warren Poems

I am not Warren.

His life touches mine only on the periphery of memory and imagination. His thoughts, hopes, disappointments, fears are mine only vicariously, as we shared together the focal points of two lives, one real, one imagined; then watched them diverge as work and image refined them to give them life and meaning.

I am not Warren, or at least no more than any poet is the voice that struggles up from the depths, off of the paper, into the minds of those who will listen. And Warren is not me.

Yet for a while—for almost two years, after the death of my father, after an increasingly severe hearing problem that threatened the stability of my life and my assumptions—Warren and I shared many midnight hours together. He listened to my fears. I listened to his stories as they formed across the computer page.

We grew to know one another.

I learned to trust him to say things I could not say for myself. He learned to trust me to swerve from my own stories and follow his when they became too powerful to fit into what I had thought to write.

I learned to understand that what he had to say reflected *me but was not me. He learned that what he had to say started in me, but rapidly became someone else. Became him.*

So I am not Warren. Warren is not me.

And these poems, called by his name, written by my hand, are neither of us, but a culmination of memories and images, hopes and fears, victories and defeats that—together—we struggled to define.

WARREN—PORTRAIT OF THE ARTIST AS A NEUROTIC

Awake at two am, waiting for the leak
he knows will come, must come
(as it has come for three long years
of nuzzling black whammy into cracks
and lifting butt-end shingles to finger
secret recesses for dampness)—

he knows the roof is sound, knows it
with the upper layerings of little grey
cells that constitute his mind—but
in the darker damper places he
knows knows *knows* that it will come
must come is fated to come and
drip drip *drip* insidious dampness
into the drywall, into the two-by-fours
that frame the window,

into the four-chambered tissues of his
waiting heart and clog the arteries
of his life
with thick white pasty sludge…
part drywall, part stucco, part
rarified adust of his melancholy fears

Warren, Dressed as a Sunbeam

pivots on a rusted children's swing
trailing clouds of golden
crepe-paper glory

twisted on seven-year shoulders; brow
cramped beneath cardboard
crown rippled by

glued-on crepe to match his robes.
Sunbeam in the Kindergarten
play, he grins into the

camera, shrugs against time-rusted links
supporting the seat that keeps
his feet from earth

WARREN SLEEPS OVER

Sleeping overnight at Cousin Cray's
Twelve-year-old Warren rolled restlessly on
Rusted springs beneath a wide
Boxelder canopy. Dew soaked
Coarse, woven blankets, chilling his feet
And legs. He shivered once, and brushed
Cray's warmth.

Overhead, Orion spun. Up the road
Gravel crunched, and headlights pinioned
Warren's hunted eyes. City-bred,
He waited heart-pent for coyote wails,
Wolf howls, owl screeches
To paint the darkness scarlet
With unfed hunger.

Cray rolled on his side. Springs grimaced
At the weight. Warren screwed his eyelids
Closed, counted to a thousand (flinching only once
When unnamed monsters buzzed his cheek);
A thousand once again, then peeked through
Half-slit lids and felt blood gorge his throat
When dawn had not yet come.

WARREN'S MOTHER BRINGS HIM WATER

Weeding at twelve, grubby-dirty-dusty
Nearly naked under California's
Sun, he kneels on scabby skin and yanks
Prickles with fingers callused and tough. Sweat

Burns his neck, burns dark hollows behind
His knees. Dirt flicks from rounded root-clumps
That choose not to die. Bermuda tendrils
Snake through rank-grown marigolds, swish

Serpentine through grass to startle him.
Break time. He stands, stretches. Angular ribs
Crescent brown flesh. Narrow hips and bone-thin
Arms show first hints of muscling to come.

She moves from shadows, pitcher in one hand,
Weeping glass outstretched. He drinks and wipes
His forehead with a filthy hand, leaving
One brown swath darker than the rest.

She stares a moment…long enough that he
Suddenly *feels* first-naked in her eyes.
He knows the thinness of his worn nylon
Shorts…his nakedness underneath. He wants

To glance down and does not. She points, her finger
Glistens from the weeping glass. "Don't wear
Those like that again." The scorching sun
Abruptly shadows to his flaming cheeks.

Warren Travels with His Father

in the
dense Montana heat, the BLM vehicle musty
and smelling of oil, sweat, and age.

Warren
skips school for those two days—two days
alone with Dad, staying in old, decaying

motels
where floors feel slick with thin linoleum and windows
glow behind crepe-paper drapes and

single
burner kitchenettes transform outdated army
C-rations into exotic feasts and

lumpy
bedframes support old-fashioned
metal springs that squawk when

Warren's
eighty pounds and Dad's one-eighty
shift. At dawn, they load the truck,

Hunker
down against an early chill, and set out for
the boondocks, Dad to hunt elusive

bench marks
and pace off invisible section lines, Warren to watch
and etch each shifting outline in

his mind,
and store them to relive once they two again
return and reassume their separate lives.

WARREN DREAMS WHILE SLEEPING OUTSIDE DURING A HEAT WAVE

shimmering July heat—coiling California heat
    settles in languid layers on browning grass
        and ripening fruit bare weeks away
from rotting. Heat twisting in serpent
    coils up weathered fence posts,
        slithering across grass-green
concrete where Warren's down mummy-bag
    twists insolently around his body like a
        discarded condom, dark
heap of darkness against grass-green
    concrete as he twists around the
        fence posts of his dreams
and shimmers brown upon glass-green
    liquid outlining her in aquarelle
        to his umber gouache
startlingly harshly opaque. She shimmers
    glass-green through water caught in
        webs of shattered glass that
slice opacity and reveal the shattering glass-green
    light layering flesh explosive shimmering
        heat of crimson aquarelle and ivory
gouache twisting in the heat of his down-bag
    where it lay ragged rumpled adolescent
        lump on grass-green concrete
shimmering in June heat—sleeping heat
    settled in layers on browning glass
        and frightening fruit.

WARREN RECALLS—MOLESTATION

rings too harshly in my memory
yet frightens even now, and echoes heartbeats
rusty, obscured;

no, it was not quite, but something
close—back then, the word did not yet
ring with panic.

I remember a new green shirt, hand-
sewn for the day; white pants tighter than
comfortable;

a bicycle pumping up the hill toward
a row of shops set well back from the road,
inviting, cool.

I remember storeroom shelves
where I was put to work—stacking boxes
of unworn shoes.

He held it up. I did not know what
it was. He called it a 'dance-belt' and
explained its use.

 "Try it on," he urged. I considered,
glanced toward a screened-in area behind
the racks of shoes.

I might have taken it if someone
(unseen, unheard except for a hidden bell)
had not entered;

when he returned, I was hard at work
stacking boxes—empty, full, I did not care,
that job was safe.

Later, he came back. He did not try
again. Instead, he talked of nervousness
and tense muscles.

I did not understand. He ran the small
machine across my shoulders, down my
sides and slat-thin ribs;

He murmured as he worked. He touched
the small machine to my crotch and smiled
a secret smile.

The hidden bell rang again. He left.
I stacked the boxes, numb and shaking,
until he closed.

 "It won't work out," he said, stripping
a handful of dollars from his wallet. "It
just won't work out."

Green shirt. White pants. Bicycle awkward
against my thighs. I struggled home. I never spoke
the ugly word.

Warren Discovers Classical Music

late one afternoon, slamming though
the front-room door, textbooks jamming

angularities against ribs pain-tight from
racing Greg the last half-block, head light

with summer heat and thirst crawling
against a throat as dry as snakeskins. First

traceries of sound slide home beneath throbbing
blood, slide with strength of cathedral stone,

carven lucencies defying centuries.
Sounds insinuate, sounds compel, prying

stone-web fingers beneath his skull, lifting
skullcap, engorging mind and soul until full

beyond endurance with its insubstantial weight.
Angularities and snakeskin thirst burst—trivial

Soap bubble memories glisten upon
Cathedral stone, tracery-fine, as he listens.

WARREN AND GREG TALK

late at
night, with Greg's kid brother snoring
damply on the living room couch and Warren

atop
the old chenille bedspread that smells
faintly of dog and sweat and pre-teen boy, and

when Greg
flicks the light off and darkness settles
like a brittle lie between them they talk of truths

unseen
because they are unseen their voices flit
like insects through the darkness—have you

ever?
do you think you would? would she?
who? when? Greg says never, no, probably

no one
would ever want him. Warren lies uncomfortably
aroused as the voices speak and wonders about loneliness.

Warren Goes Camping

At seventeen, a week after graduation,
Warren walked out for the first
and last

Time without speaking to her. He climbed
in the front seat of Greg's puke-green,
time-scarred

convertible and drove off without looking
back. Only a short trip—three days
in the

Sierras with Greg, over her express wishes
but what the hell he was almost an adult
and now

on the winding roads with the wind skimming
through his hair and his eyes squinting
against

the slanting light what the hell he would look
forward not backward toward the dark
front door

slammed behind him. They pitched camp along
the rocky edges of a lake he could not name
not then

not now but the marge extended for a hundred
yards between skimpy pines and murky
water

enough for the two-man tent they crammed their
gear into that first night before they caught
a fire

and grilled still frozen hot dogs from the cooler.
Greg slept nude—Warren wore pj's that first
night. They

hiked during the heat of the day, severing spider
threads with uncanny skill where they hung
like chains

from already desiccated weeds. Greg shucked off
his shorts and shoes and shirt and skinned
naked

into the lake. Warren followed, rushed and thumping
and fearful—but who was there, a hundred
miles from

nowhere who could see or tell or care. Greg sliced
like a knifeblade cutting into glinting water;
Warren

splashed and floundered before he caught his breath
and stroked and surface-dived, reaching for a
bottom

he knew was there but that he would never reach. Two
Days passed. Late the third night he re-opened the
Dark door.

Warren Opens a Closet in the Attic

When Warren woke that day
To stifling air that settled like a mask
Of flesh across his face,

He knew the attic waited—
A beast crouching in heat and dark and filth
That dared his wary approach.

But he rose, showered,
Shaved, munched a piece of whole-wheat toast
Smeared with blood-red jam,

And mounted step by step
The waiting beast. He swept grey joists until
Wood gleamed dark;

He packed old cast-off
Clothing, shoes, toys, and Christmas wrap
Saved from World War II

By his grandmother—foil
Wrap fly-spotted, mouse-nibbled among
Gray wreathes and mildewed bells.

He shoved aside three crates
(Once useful, he was sure, now bare and dry)
And found the closet door.

The knob was tarnished brass,
The lock wept closed by corrosion green-slime thick
Caked on the buckled face.

He touched the knob, twisted
Once, three times—knelt back upon his heels,
Then pried a bar against

Warped wood and pressed. It groaned,
He groaned a humid counterpart that started
In his gut and tore his throat.

The door sprang open, nearly
Smashing Warren's knee. The black inside,
Web-hung, stared out.

He breathed. The darkness rippled
In response. He stepped back—the darkness
Rippled once again.

He moved beneath the lintel…
And saw himself, fly-spotted, warped and grey
In the swollen mirror

That faced the closet back.
He stood a long time, staring at the face,
Shaggy with waves of dust,

That stared wide-eyed
Out at him. He closed the door and braced
It locked with three large

Empty cartons, bare
And dry; descended wood-plank stairs, step
By step; showered, dressed

In clean white tennis shorts,
In tight-taut T-shirt—combed his hair
And thought no more

About the brace-locked attic door.

Warren Returns To the Homestead

Beyond dim, time-worn crests of sage—
Grey-green outcasts in the shade of Chimney Rock—
Stretch Elba's sheltered, hedge-quartered fields.
To the south, the gash of Hollow Creek
Etches aspen-burnished mountain flanks above the farms
North toward the Albion Road.

Gravel-strewn, the curve of Albion Road
Severs narrow arteries of sage,
Then cuts the western edge of Grandpa's farm
Near where it sleeps beneath Chimney Rock,
Near where the algae-gutted basin that was Hollow Creek
Widens to irrigate dry fields.

Once, hard red winter wheat bearded the fields,
Whiskered the eastern edge of old Albion Road
And curled across the valley to the mouth of Hollow Creek;
Once, one-room cabins nested in cups edged with sage
And rode the slopes across from Chimney Rock—
Once, when Great-great-grandpa settled here to farm.

For decades now, no new folk have come to farm;
They buy the red brick houses…but ignore wide fields
Fallow and neglected in the scowl of Chimney Rock;
Slick RV trailers glide the curve of Albion Road
Where horse-drawn wagons rattled through thick sage
To picnics up Hollow Creek.

It's been years since people drove up Hollow Creek,
Since fields were sown on Grandpa's farm;
And what was garden then, now repossessed by sage

And sego lilies and russet paintbrush dotting fields
Alien and cold against the curve of Albion Road,
Beneath the snaggletooth of Chimney Rock.

No one nowadays notices Chimney Rock
Gazing stonily up Hollow Creek
From vacant heights above the Albion Road;
In the valley, shadows leap, farm to dying farm,
Scatter twilight-seeds upon dead fields—
Wombs of bone-white, weaving sage.

He drives beneath Chimney Rock, looks across the farm,
Winds up Hollow Creek, tromps new-mown fields—
In memory. Albion Road bisects grey-green shades of sage.

WARREN REMEMBERS THE CHICKEN COOP

After thirty years, the dry-dank musty stench
Of feathers rotting, layered in acrid dung,
Fades

To soft nostalgic folds. The coop (once bedroom
In the house where Warren's mother first saw life)
Squats

Again beneath a scorching August sun.
Inside that stifling womb, Rhode Island Reds
Laid

Clutches in straw-strewn pine-frame boxes. Some sat
Amid the stench to harvest chicks. Others
Caught

The mote-thick air with stubby wings and, squawking,
Flapped from lime-caked perches on the wall and
Made

Their gooney-landings in the dust each time
He squeaked the ragged screendoor open. There they
Fought

To peck at him—it seemed—as if he were
The morsel of the day for beaks that should have
Played

For worms in dusty outdoor yards. But here
Enclosed, they fed and bred and laid their eggs and
Sought

Small, mindless battles in the dark. Their lives
Became miasmal ghosts of smell that should have
Stayed

Embedded in dim, fly-specked shreds of paper—
Exhalations surfacing like fungal
Rot;

But after thirty years, the musty stench
Of feathers molding, layered in acrid dung,
Fades.

WARREN RELIVES SIERRA FIRES

Thirty-three years ago blackened skies
Over John Barrett Elementary
At noon. The sun hung, less than a tarnished nickel,
Hidden in sheaths of floating ash,
Air hot and heavy from flames a hundred miles
Away, breath aching-still and sedentary
While pupils peered uneasily through wire-webbed
Glass at midday darkness, eyes awash
From acrid stinging…for the moment, lights
Were switched on, windows shut—cautionary
Actions to protect students. All might have passed
In eerie darkness and silence—had not the gash
Of sound echoed along corridors, cries
That ripped the solemn stillness…incendiary
Cry more startling than the flat black sheet
Of sky.
    "The end of the world has come!"
                                    She splashed
Daubs of sound as she whirled once, eyes
Staring-white, cheeks white, face scary-
Stiff—she screamed again into the sepulchre
Our room had suddenly become…then dashed
Beyond his sight, into the darkness, surprise
Warbling behind her. One boy stifled a wary
Gasp; another hiccoughed softly into
Cupped hands. Somewhere, the voice crashed
Against concrete walls, rose and died.
Black silence melted from the sky to bury
John Barrett Elementary in residues of flames.
Ash etched reddened eyes with prickling flashes.

Warren Plants a New Garden

Digging beds for small tomato plants
Yesterday, buried to the fingertips
In earth

Both dark and black, he happened on
A smooth, clear roundness—
Relic

Of last fall's harvest, slumbering until
Next month's warmth should touch
And wake—

A new potato, unseen, warding soil,
Keeping faith until the new spring's
Seeding.

Warren Answers a Telephone Call from Greg

Sixth grade, like the dinosaurs, had long since
    passed into history. Names, faces, laughter
        at silly jokes no one fully understood—
            all had died
in tumultuous time-worls as cataclysmic as a
    comet slipping near enough the face of
        Earth to plant a killing kiss on her
            wrinkled flesh
and destroy in the passing. So sixth grade—thirty
    years long passed. And more than five since
        Greg had called last time. Even so,
            With one call
Greg transformed time—the half-forgotten timbre
    of a long-remembered voice distorted by wires,
        resurrected dinosaurs, recalled sixth grade from
            history.

        At midnight, Warren contemplated
    Greg's visit…the first in half a decade.
No fear, no worry—no tempting cunning fate
        With expectations that could fade
    At one wrong word, a pause one breath
Too long. Warren sat in midnight's shade
        And rolled slick memories beneath
    Blunt fingertips, pressed grey keys
To imprison their slickness in a sheath
        Of safety. Words replaced the *he*
    That Warren knew and lost too late
To find a new. A Greg would come and be.

Warren Harvests a Beefsteak Tomato

as large as his clenched fist. He has waited,
watered, watched warden

while pests barged their ways through knots
of melon garden

thick to assault tomato bastions. One green bulb
fist thick strains to

red halting through saffron. Tomorrow he will
snap its grainy

stem and carry it to a sunny windowsill. It will
ripen—or so he hopes—

to rich berry redness. In the darkness a snail skims
thick, orange, ropy skin.

Warren Considers Patriphobia

Perhaps
I should condemn my father be-
 cause he never beat me as a child,

 never
fondled me in the privacy
 of bathtub or of showerstall

 never
darkened the blackness of my bed-
 room with a naked midnight visit

 never
screamed out my inadequacies
 to an evil, eavesdropping world

 never
suffered me to deviate from
 stark standards of action and of will;

 BUT left
me isolated and lonely
 and responsible for my choices;

 and I
cannot look back on a childhood
 designed to expiate my errors

 by giv-
ing up my agency and blam-
 ing him for molding me in my sins.

WARREN, IN THERAPY TODAY

In therapy today I learned
to say
    ashamed
        embarrassed
            envious
and see…

ghosts haunting web-hung rafters
trapped for memories like
flies flesh-wrapped and plump
pumping life-blood to fang-flames
    ashamed

ghosts lining dim-stretched halls
palled with pale shades of fear
sheer and biting, waiting on the joke
the poke the laugh the harassment
    embarrassed

ghosts unborn infiltrating joys—
toys taut-wound and tense
pretense unveiled and bitter loss
tossed unnoticed to dead dust
        envious

I see…

In therapy today I learned
to say

WARREN EVALUATES THE EFFECTS OF ARIPIPRAZOLE

Words grow hauntingly,
Roll half-tauntingly from the mind
Where once, not long ago,
Image poured and metaphor
Fused meaning with high passion—
And also darkled shadows, fear, and dread.

Instead of rocket highs and
Depth-plumbed lows,
Widely barren plains, unbroken now
By crest or depth, unfurrowed in the
Lassitude of listlessness,
Numbed and dumbed and stilled.

To walk is easier thus.
Each step-by-step level and unruffled.
Horizons no longer loom. Twilights
Linger until the moon herself sleeps settled.
And dawn creeps slowly on until she
Merges unbeknownst with noon.
And thus it is. And is. And is.

And whether that is good,
I do not know.

WARREN'S MOTHER SELLS THE HOUSE

Two years after the burial, she seemed
Shrunken, a witch doctor's shriveled case
Pressing upon the kernel-core. She leaned

Harder on him now, as if to erase
Earlier despite that masqueraded
As ice. Now, pared down to sudden base

Emotions, she shrank more. Each day, unaided,
She assaulted closet corners, gritted teeth
When shadows engulfed memory and braided

Where the husband-father lurked beneath
His death. Warren watched her shrink, unable
To do more than shoulder weights, breathe

The stale scent of workshop dust, or sweat
Beneath stiff attic heat. He could not touch
Her loss or staunch the acrid tears that wet

Warm cheeks he knew as ice. He felt a clutch
Of sorrow, could watch from outside in as she
Worked through forty years. There was much

He would not know about their lives—he
Only watched as she pressed rough fingertips
Against a paper blotched and creased, tea-

Dark with age…and wonder what sharp slips
Of fear she felt. She changed. He changed. They
Sold the house. He made the stuttering trips

With her ghost, watched her try to lay
The husband/father quietly behind.
More passed between them on the final day

Than in his nearly thirty years. The rind
Was stripped away. Alone except for him,
She left the house—his childhood—behind.

Warren Says Farewell to His Father's Ghost

Late, late
At night—past midnight easily, but long before
Dawn broke its fever over unmown grass, Warren

Crept the
Dim hallway pitched black beneath the cold, dead
Bulbs. His fingers twitched to touch the switch, but thought

Gave way
To feeling, and the hall remained in blackness. He
Felt his way toward his study, passing canted doors that harbored

All that
Was of goodness in his life. They slept. He heard
Soft patterings of breath. The rustle of a midnight sheet flung back

Against
Oppressive heat. Low murmurs of electric fans
Struggling vainly. He sweat. His breath rasped harshly,

Scented
Distantly with dinner's pungent shade. He reached his
Study, pulled the door to as silently as if he and the door were

Lost thoughts
Sinking far beneath cold, naked memories. He took paper,
Pen—ignoring for the while the ice-grey monitor and printer

Sitting
Primed upon the desk. This time paper, pen…physical
Motion of hand and wrist brushing fibers once living, now

Long dead.
Words flowed faster than he had hoped. Memories…
Sounds…Pictures…A life rebounding images on white-washed

Plaster
Inside his head. He wrote. Dawn flushed across the
Grass, staining August-withered lawns the pink of party

Ribbons
As he wrote of life and death. He stopped. Stretched.
Muscles sheathing spine and ribs ached. Joints cracked like

Winter
Ice when new-born waters swirl beneath in jets that
Lead past spawning grounds to merge with ocean swells and

Generate
Anew. He rubbed his eyes. The words remained, graphite
Grey against ivory. Darkness spilled across the light, making

The light
Glow stronger. The sun broke his window sill. The paper
Glowed the pink of party ribbons. He folded the paper carefully

And laid
It in the binding of the Bible his Father gave him on a
Christmas long years gone by and almost lost. He closed the

Leather
Book. His fingers felt small nubbles as they passed along the
Spine, caressed its softness, then slid the book again into its place
   upon

The shelf.

INDEX OF FIRST LINES

A roiling tumbleweed, propelled by west—: 46
A thousand wives lie close to heart: 19
After thirty years, the dry-dank musty stench: 180
Along this stretch of beach cold sands sing: 154
Already cold and stiff by the time I arrived: 86
An evanescent spider filigrees: 104
And Plums. Apples, even, on the tree: 105
And when She died her children slid: 78
Applebuds assault slick pewter mist: 139
As large as his clenched fist. He has waited: 185
At seventeen, a week after graduation: 174
Awake at half past six on Sunday morning—: 85
Awake at two am, waiting for the leak: 163
Banked Morning Glories robe our weathered fence: 140
Bathing in the great tin tub: 38
Beyond dim, time-worn crests of sage—: 178
Brittleness in light—: 52
By all accounts my great-great-great: 22
Cast up with just their jock: 118
Come fall, we'd gather with the rest: 156
Digging beds for small tomato plants: 183
Do not ripen on the tree but wait: 143
Each time I stalk the valley's graveled road: 76
Even now the house remembers: 32
Feet splayed, he sits: 27
First, rise early, while the first July: 48
Flutter-whirr: 110

For six weeks after, she remained: 25
Gaunt ravaged bareskull: 97
God not yet: 146
Grey grey cataclysmic: 153
Haunts me even now—ghostly chords that reach: 63
He is not in the valley: 88
Homeless I sit, patient, at the corner: 123
I am stone: 106
I find what I seek—: 95
I have seen the mountain glazed with: 136
I have Time too much, too much—: 133
I held him once in my single hand: 70
I owe my father much: 94
I roam summer paths—: 47
I saw you once…and last: 129
I was six: 28
Imagination invites me to hear: 138
In Grandmother's attic: 36
In the / dense Montana heat, the BLM vehicle musty: 167
In the first house we owned we: 42
In the stone chapel (cold stone: 60
In therapy today I learned: 187
In those Sputnik days when farmers' sons: 54
Into the forest, woods, copse (a word that: 62
It's easy now to read about them—distanced: 102
It's hot and sweaty work: 96
June always comes as a surprise: 101
Late at / night, with Greg's kid brother snoring: 173
Late one afternoon, slamming though: 172
Late, late / At night—past midnight easily, but long before: 191
Late-set apples half-grown wither: 144
Milton felt no frost when Damon died: 124
Miscarry is a false name: 90
Noon—at 20°—and the branches of leafless: 45
November wind—and ice behind the promises—: 145
On the raw canvas of words, images form: 127
Perhaps / I should condemn my father be-: 186

Picking iris on a day: 141
Piece by piece I deconstruct my: 131
Pivots on a rusted children's swing: 164
Remind me—inexplicably—of Elba: 64
Rings too harshly in my memory: 170
Shimmering July heat—coiling California heat: 169
Sixth grade, like the dinosaurs, had long since: 184
Sleeping overnight at Cousin Cray's: 165
SO Amy [*Aimee*, 'beloved', broke: 65
Some words must be whispered after dark: 91
Sputnik was up. Grade school students saw *that* film: 57
Thank you: 100
That year was wet, with summer storms that blew: 58
That's what he said, I swear: 117
The irrigation ditch lies dead: 148
The river passes, gurgling its thoughts: 158
The road, still roughly graveled, drops the length: 67
The winds blew forty below: 50
The winter I turned twelve: 43
Then, at ten, (younger and smaller than all: 126
They hatched today. Last night: 149
They told me that my cougar was only a child's silly dream: 41
They've covered rough-cut logs with: 74
Thirty-three years ago blackened skies: 182
Thunder rumbled through the valley: 31
Tin-: 121
Today a radio talk-show host: 83
Today while I worried: 92
Two years after the burial, she seemed: 189
Warm bread broken into warm cream-: 35
Was a climax forty years ago—: 29
WE breathe in separate hemi-: 98
We drove past my great-grandfather's place: 72
We fished for crawdads from the old plank bridge: 34
We rode behind the tractor on the hay wagon—: 61
We stare he and I strangers faceless voiceless bound: 120
Weeding at twelve, grubby-dirty-dusty: 166

Weeding in the poetry beds…pottering: 157
When my eldest rested long, strong fingers on my head and: 87
When she died, they found the box: 69
When Warren woke that day: 176
While two rooms away: 108
Words grow hauntingly: 188

INDEX OF TITLES

1959: 54
After Chores: 35
After Thirty Years of Teachings: 126
Alone, in the Chapel, at the Console: 95
An Act of Contrition: 46
Anamnesis I: 74
Anamnesis II: 76
Applebuds Assault Slick Pewter Mist: 139
Apricots This Year: 105
At the Crick: 34
Bank of Virgins : 117
Bartlett Pears: 143
Bathing in the Great Tin Tub: 38
Betrayal: 41
Beyond the Harvest: 144
Bud Died: 92
Cambria Shoreline: 146
Childless: 90
Choosing Irises: 141
Clapboard Memory: 72
Classical Music: 63
Cleaning the Garage: 104
Continuity: 158
Damon Again: 124
Entire Unto Himself: 86
Father-Child: 87
First Apricot: 101

For Grace Isabella: 129
For My Son: 70
Free Agency: 85
Fuchsias and Bleeding-Hearts: 64
Going a Mile a Minute: 29
Grandmother's Attic: 36
He is Not in the Valley: 88
Her Journals: 69
Heritage: 32
How to Make Raspberry Syrup: 48
I Have Seen the Mountain: 134
I Have Time: 133
I Owe My Father Much: 94
I, Homeless: 123
Into Bread: 60
Into the Forest: 62
It's Hot and Sweaty Work: 96
Janusaries: 98
Just to Say: 100
Legacy I: 22
Legacy II: 78
M: 19
Making Love at Midnight: 108
Maternity Home: 25
Melmac: 50
Monolith: The Tale and the Teller: 65
Morning Bells: 138
Morning Glories: 140
Nestling: 149
Off-Shore Flow: 153
On First Seeing My Photograph as a Six-Month Child: 27
Portrait of the Artist on the Verge of Middle Age: 127
Quilting: 131
Remembering the First Photograph of a Survivor: 97
Restoration: 145
Ritual: 120
Shipwrecked Among the Channel Islands: 118

Sledding in Montana: 43
Snow Draperies: 45
Sparks: 121
Summer Stanzas: 47
Summer, 1953: 28
The House We Owned: 42
The Irrigation Ditch Lies Dead: 148
The Passing of the Old Guard: 31
The Pigeon Woman in Cooley Park: 110
The Road: 67
The Tractor: 61
The Tyranny of Equilibrium: 154
They Had a Dream: 1959: 58
Today: 83
Tornado Weather in Montana, 1959: 52
Tulips: 103
Walnut Harvest: 156
Warren and Greg Talk: 173
Warren Answers a Telephone Call from Greg: 184
Warren Considers Patriphobia: 186
Warren Discovers Classical Music: 172
Warren Dreams While Sleeping Outside During a Heat Wave: 169
Warren Evaluates the Effects of Aripiprazole: 188
Warren Goes Camping: 174
Warren Harvests a Beefsteak Tomato: 185
Warren Opens a Closet in the Attic: 176
Warren Plants a New Garden: 183
Warren Recalls—Molestation: 170
Warren Relives Sierra Fires: 182
Warren Remembers the Chicken Coop: 180
Warren Returns to the Homestead: 178
Warren Says Farewell to His Father's Ghost: 191
Warren Sleeps Over: 165
Warren Travels with His Father: 167
Warren, Dressed as a Sunbeam: 164
Warren, in Therapy Today: 187
Warren's Mother Brings Him Water: 166

Warren's Mother Sells the House: 189
Warren—Portrait of the Artist as a Neurotic: 163
We Built Forts: 57
Weeding in the Poetry Beds: 157
Whispers: 91
Wind and Stone: 106

About the Author

MICHAEL R. COLLINGS is an Emeritus Professor of English at Seaver College, Pepperdine University, where he directed the Creative Writing Program for over two decades. He has published multiple volumes of poetry, novels, short fiction, and scholarly studies of such contemporary writers as Stephen King, Orson Scott Card, Dean R. Koontz, and Piers Anthony. His most recent works include *Singer of Lies*, a science-fiction novel; *The Art and Craft of Poetry*; *In the Void: Poems of Science Fiction, Myth and Fantasy, and Horror*; and a Book of Mormon epic, *The Nephiad.* He is now retired and lives in his native state of Idaho.

www.ingramcontent.com/pod-product-compliance
Lightning Source LLC
LaVergne TN
LVHW041618070426
835507LV00008B/320